FRONTISPIECE

Some representatives of the Primates of to-day. (A) A Tree-
shrew (*Tupaia*). (B) A Lemur (*Galago*). (C) A Tarsier (*Tarsius*).
(D) A Macaque Monkey (*Macaca*). (E) A Gibbon (*Hylobates*).
(F) A Chimpanzee (*Pan*). Drawings by Maurice Wilson.

HISTORY
OF THE
PRIMATES

AN INTRODUCTION
TO THE STUDY OF
FOSSIL MAN

BY

Sir WILFRID LE GROS CLARK, F.R.S.
EMERITUS PROFESSOR OF ANATOMY IN
THE UNIVERSITY OF OXFORD

TENTH EDITION

TRUSTEES OF THE
BRITISH MUSEUM (NATURAL HISTORY)
LONDON: 1970

First Edition	–	–	1949
Second Edition	–	–	1950
Third Edition	–	–	1953
Fourth Edition	–	–	1954
Fifth Edition	–	–	1956
Sixth Edition	–	–	1958
Seventh Edition	–	–	1960
Eighth Edition	–	–	1962
Ninth Edition	–	–	1965
Tenth Edition	–	–	1970

Publication No. 539

Standard Book No. 56500539 1

Printed and bound in England by
STAPLES PRINTERS LIMITED
at their Kettering, Northants, establishment.

PREFACE

The ninth edition was emended to include advances in our knowledge of the history of the primates yielded by recent researches in Africa. The text figures were remade and increased in number and a new Time Scale added. The present edition differs only in that the Time Scale incorporates the most recent revisions in the estimates of absolute time.

H. W. BALL
Keeper of Palaeontology

19 *August,* 1970

CONTENTS

HISTORY OF THE PRIMATES
AN INTRODUCTION TO THE STUDY OF FOSSIL MAN

Man in the Scheme of Evolution

In his bodily structure Man shows such remarkable resemblances to the lower animals that it now seems astonishing to us that his kinship with them should ever have been seriously controverted. His skull and skeleton are composed of the same bony elements, his muscular system is made up of identical muscles disposed in the same general pattern, his heart and blood-vessels are constructed on exactly the same plan, and even his brain (though it is more elaborate) is made of the same kind of nervous tissue and built up on a foundation of the same basic elements. Anatomically, therefore, Man is simply one of the animals. But we can go further than that. We can say that he belongs to the group of vertebrate animals called "mammals", for he shares with these all their distinctive features, such as warm-bloodedness, the hairiness of the skin, the structure of the teeth and jaws, the design of the breathing apparatus, the method of giving birth to young, of suckling them after birth, and so forth. Mammals, again, are subdivided into a number of separate groups, or Orders, each of which is characterized by a certain combination of distinctive anatomical features. For example, there are the Carnivora (including lions, tigers, wolves, badgers and the like), the Cheiroptera or bats (in all of which the forelimbs have become modified in the same curious way so as to become converted into wings), the Perissodactyla or odd-toed ungulates (including horses, rhinoceroses and tapirs), and the Artiodactyla or even-toed ungulates (including deer, cattle, pigs, camels and giraffes). The mammalian Order to which Man naturally belongs (by reason of his anatomical structure) is called the Primates, and it also includes apes, monkeys, lemurs and certain other smaller creatures.

THE CLASSIFICATION OF ANIMALS AND ITS EVOLUTIONARY IMPLICATION

As just indicated, each of the Orders of the mammals is defined by certain anatomical characters which their members possess in common, and which serve to distinguish them from other Orders. By the same sort of criteria, each Order can be subdivided into separate sub-Orders, each sub-Order into families, and each family into genera, and each genus is made up of individual species. A satisfactory definition of the term " species " still defies the ingenuity of the zoologist, but, as a rough approximation, it may be said to consist of a homogeneous category of individuals closely resembling each other (except for relatively minor variations, such as those of moderate differences in size and colour), and usually capable of interbreeding freely and producing fully fertile offspring.

The relatively minor variations often shown by different geographical groups belonging to one species may lead to the recognition of a further subdivision into sub-species, or races, but such varieties tend to grade into each other, and also (as just indicated) they can usually interbreed freely. For example, the different races of mankind may be regarded as sub-species of the species *Homo sapiens*, and some of the varieties of domestic dog as sub-species of the species *Canis familiaris*. As a matter of fact, it is not always easy to decide in all cases whether different varieties are just sub-species, or whether they are sufficiently distinct to be called separate species. Some zoologists have in the past argued that the different races of mankind are really to be regarded as different species, though it is now almost universally agreed that, by the usual criteria, such a distinction is unwarranted. On the other hand, there is every reason to suppose that sub-species are potentially species in the making, that is, they may represent actual stages in the process of evolutionary diversification, and, if this is the case, it is to be expected that the one type of category will tend to grade into the other.

The hierarchical system of zoological classification, whereby the smaller units with common anatomical characters are grouped together into larger and larger categories, owes its origin to the great naturalist, Linnaeus, in the middle of the eighteenth century, and it was initially designed simply as a convenience for cataloguing and ready identification. It was an attempt to reduce to some sort of system and order the apparent confusion in the diversity of plant and animal life, as a necessary preliminary to their systematic study. But, particularly since the time of Darwin, it has come to have a far more profound significance. For one of the essential implications of the evolutionary hypothesis is that fundamental resemblances in anatomical structure betoken an actual blood-relationship.

One might have supposed that there would have been nothing very startling in this idea when it was first seriously entertained by biologists, for it was generally recognized that local varieties or races of a single species might be the result of a diversification produced by different environmental influences, so that differences in size, colour and other superficial traits need not obscure the fact that all these varieties were originally derived from the same stock. Thus, naturalists were quite ready to accept the view that the different breeds of domestic dog might have been produced by a process of gradual diversification from a common stock represented (probably) by the wolf. The different sizes, proportions and colours of the various breeds do not conceal the fundamental similarities in anatomical details which show that they have a common origin. But, at the time of the Darwinian controversy, the idea of the fixity and immutability of the different animal and plant *species* was very tenaciously held by biologists generally, quite apart from the fact that some of them were no doubt influenced by the biblical story of the creation. It was largely because of this (and also because the relationship of Man to lower animals was brought into the problem) that Darwin's " Origin of Species " met with such severe opposition from certain quarters.

Natural Selection

Darwin's claim to fame in the history of evolutionary theory is not merely that he amassed overwhelming evidence that the various species of organisms have arisen by a process of gradual evolutionary differentiation from common ancestral forms, but he was the first to give a rational and well documented explanation of how such evolution had occurred. It is common knowledge, of course, that animal and plant breeders can develop new varieties by artificially selecting from their stocks individuals which show novel features, isolating them from the rest of the stock, and crossing them with each other. If such novel features are the result of some change in the hereditary particles in the germ cells, that is to say, if they are the result of what biologists call "mutations", they will be transmitted from parent to offspring, and thus by artificial selection and careful breeding a completely new variety of animal or plant can be established. Darwin showed quite conclusively that there is also a process of "natural selection" going on all the time which is also effective in the production of new types. Put baldly, natural selection (as it is now generally accepted) can be described as follows. All living things show a tendency to vary, and heritable variations (each of which may originate from one or more mutations) are transmitted from one generation to another. Those individuals affected by heritable variations which give them a definite advantage over their fellows will be more likely to survive in the struggle for existence, and to reproduce their kind. The less favoured individuals, on the other hand, will tend to die out. Thus, in the course of many generations, the species will tend to show a gradual change in the direction of a more perfect adaptation to the environment in which it exists.

A simple example will serve to illustrate this general principle. It is known, from a study of the fossil record, that during the evolution of horses their limbs became gradually perfected more and more as instruments of speed while, at the same time, their molar teeth became more complicated and so more efficient as grinding mechanisms. It is easy to understand that those individuals which could run faster would be more likely to escape from enemies and therefore would be more likely to survive and reproduce their kind, while in the same way those with more efficient molar teeth would be able to make better use of the food-stuffs at their disposal and would therefore be more likely to survive in times of scarcity. Consequently, whenever in the course of evolution hereditary changes occurred which led to improvements in the limbs or molar teeth, these would tend to be perpetuated, while the less efficient mechanisms would tend to die out. In other words, this process of the "survival of the fittest" would lead "automatically" to a gradual change in the anatomical make-up of the species, which is simply another way of saying it would result in evolution.

THE INDIRECT EVIDENCE FOR THE PRINCIPLE OF EVOLUTION

What, now, is the essential evidence for the evolutionary concept? We cannot here enter into a discussion of all of this evidence, but it may be convenient for readers if some of it is very briefly summarized. Let us, in the first place, consider the kind of *indirect* evidence which ultimately led to the establishment of evolution as a biological principle. To begin with, there is the clear evidence that geographically isolated groups of one species may become differentiated to form separate sub-species as the result of modifications related to the particular environments in which they live. If it is once admitted that local races can be produced in this way, then it seems natural to infer that the differentiation of species has occurred in the same manner, particularly since there are many cases in which it is impossible to decide whether two contrasting types are to be regarded only as different sub-species, or as two separate species. Then there is the evidence of comparative anatomy, which becomes particularly clear when employing the methods of classification to which we have already referred. In so far as members of the same group possess certain anatomical features in common, a unity of design, it is reasonable to infer that they are genetically related (that is to say, they have a true blood-relationship), and the closer the similarities, presumably the closer the relationship.

It is often possible to arrange members of a common group in a graded series which strongly suggests an actual scale of evolutionary development. For example, in the Primates (see below, p. 28), such a series may be constructed by comparing, in order, Man, chimpanzee, monkey, tarsier, lemur and tree-shrew (see Frontispiece). Here (as will become more clearly apparent later) we seem to have a number of graded links through which the bodily structure of Man is connected with that of small mammals of quite a lowly appearance. It must not be inferred, of course, that Man was actually derived from a chimpanzee ancestor, or that a monkey ever developed from the sort of lemur which exists to-day. The various members of the Primates which exist to-day are all the terminal products of so many diverging lines of evolution; they are not in any way to be taken to represent a *linear* sequence of evolution. What a series of this kind does indicate is that, apart altogether from extinct fossil forms, there are connecting links o*f an approximate kind* between Man and lower mammals; it also suggests in a very general way the sort of transitional forms which may have occurred in an evolutionary development of Man from lower mammals.

The supposition that the various forms of animal life in existence to-day have been derived from ancestral types by a gradual process of evolutionary modification is further reinforced, from the study of comparative anatomy, by the frequent discovery of vestigial organs and structures. For example, modern horses have only one functional toe, the hoof, in each foot, but remnants of other toes still exist under the skin as small splinters of bone which apparently serve no function. It seems possible to explain these remnants only by supposing that horses have been derived from an ancestral stock in which there were several toes, and that all but one of these have been lost by a process of evolutionary modification. Attached to the human ear is a series of small rudimentary muscles which appear to be functionless. Again, their presence is hardly explicable unless we suppose they represent the remnants of active muscles which, in some early ancestral form, were capable of moving the ear as they do in most lower mammals to-day. The little nodules of bone embedded in the floor of the human pelvis (forming the "coccyx") can, it seems, only be the remains of caudal vertebrae or tail bones, from which it is to be inferred that somewhere in the pedigree of the human stock were tailed ancestors. The careful dissection of certain kinds of snake will reveal inconspicuous rudiments of limbs, which are only explicable by the assumption of evolutionary descent from limbed ancestors. Such examples of vestiges might be multiplied almost indefinitely. No one can doubt that the vestigial relics of eyes in animals such as moles or cave fish are the remains of organs whose function has in the distant past been lost in adaptation to peculiar habits of life. In precisely the same way, other vestigial structures are only to be explained satisfactorily by postulating a similar evolutionary process.

Another line of convincing evidence for the evolutionary concept is derived from the study of embryology—that is, the process of development of the individual from a fertilized germ cell, and the following are a few examples of this type of evidence. The embryos of all mammals (including Man) pass through a stage of development during which a foundation of gill arches is laid down in the neck region, precisely similar to that which, in fishes, finally leads to the establishment of functional gills. But in the mammalian embryo, as development proceeds, the elements of these gill arches become completely re-arranged so as to form, not the gills for which it seems certain they were originally intended, but structures which are more suitable for animals which live on land. In some mammals, such as the sheep, there is no collar-bone in the skeleton, and yet in the embryo the rudiment of this bone does put in a brief appearance, only to disappear again. Although in baleen whales there are no teeth, tooth germs actually develop in the whale embryo, but they never become functionally mature. At a certain stage in the development of a human embryo, the blood-vessels of the limbs are arranged in a pattern which is characteristic of many lower mammals. But the pattern becomes subsequently re-arranged in a new pattern, which is more suitable for limbs of human structure. Now, it will certainly be agreed that all these phenomena (and many more examples of the same sort could be enumerated) are quite meaningless unless they are simply due to the inheritance from ancestral forms of structures which have disappeared or undergone some modification as the result of a gradual evolutionary process. Their transient persistence in the embryo, even when they are no longer present in the adult, is an expression of the astonishing conservatism of the genetic basis of anatomical structures, as the result of which their traces may still be detected millions of years after they have ceased to have any function.

TRACING THE EVOLUTIONARY HISTORY OF MAN

Let us first consider the sort of indirect evidence which is available for inferences concerning the problem of the evolution of Man. In the commonly accepted scheme for the

classification of mammals, drawn up by Dr. G. G. Simpson of
Harvard University, Man is grouped with his nearest living
relatives, the anthropoid apes, in the same Superfamily,
Hominoidea.   He shares with the large anthropoid apes
(gorilla, chimpanzee and orang utan) a remarkable combination of distinctive anatomical features, and it would be
difficult to explain such resemblances except on the basis
of genetic relationship, with the implication that Man
and the anthropoid apes have descended from a common
ancestor in the remote past.   On the other hand, Man and
the large anthropoid apes have each developed their own
specializations, which is some cases tend to obscure the
similarities in fundamental structures.   For example, the
human brain is much more elaborately developed than the
ape brain (though constructed on the same plan), and the
common ancestor of apes and Man must presumably have
had a brain not more highly developed than that of the
former.   Again, the large apes have become rather highly
specialized for swinging about the trees in their arboreal life
by the excessively powerful development of the arms, and a
tendency to a shrinkage or atrophy of the thumb, while
Man, in this respect, has retained a more primitive and generalized type of arm.   Hence it may be inferred that the common ancestor would almost certainly not show the arboreal
adaptations in the upper limb developed to the same degree
as they are in the large anthropoid apes of to-day.
    Another striking contrast between Man and ape is the
great development in the latter of long and powerful canine
teeth, used as weapons in attack and defence.   On the other
hand, in Man the canine teeth have no special functions—
they form part of the same series with the front biting teeth
or incisors, and are used in just the same way.   But, in this
case, there is definite evidence that the human canine teeth
have indeed undergone some reduction in their later evolutionary history.   For example, even to-day they still retain
long and powerful roots out of proportion to those of adjacent
teeth, and out of proportion also to the requirements for
strength in the functions which they now perform.   Further,
in some people they are pointed and projecting in a manner
which certainly suggests that they once had their own special
functions.   But while it may thus be inferred that in the
common ancestor of Man and ape the canine teeth were defi-

nitely more powerful and projecting than they are in modern Man, it seems probable that they were not so strongly developed as they are in the modern large apes since, in the latter, their excessive development has led to a complex of specializations in the adjacent teeth, and in the skull and jaws, which have been avoided in Man.

Lastly, in association with the habit of standing and walking in the erect posture, the human foot has undergone a considerable degree of specialization in the relative enlargement and immobility of the big toe.   Yet a dissection of the foot shows that the big toe is still provided with all the necessary muscular elements which have been developed in apes to provide it with highly mobile and grasping functions (somewhat in the same manner as a thumb).   It seems reasonable to infer that this musculature is found in the human foot simply because it once served similar functions in human ancestors (though perhaps not to the degree shown in the arboreally adapted modern apes).

These examples will be sufficient to show that, by comparing the anatomical characters of all the members of the Hominoidea one by one, it is possible to make certain theoretical postulates regarding the anatomical structure of their common ancestor.   But it must be realized that such postulates are only approximate and tentative, for there are some complicating factors.   One of these is the phenomenon of "parallel evolution," that is, the evolutionary development of the same feature in two groups of animals independently.   It is known, on the evidence of fossils, that this does occur, and clearly it may lead to anatomical resemblances which are in a sense fortuitous, and are thus not indicative of close affinity in the ordinarily accepted sense of the phrase.   On the other hand, even resemblances based on parallel evolution may be interpreted as indicating an *ultimate* relationship, in so far as they are an expression of a well-known evolutionary principle that the same results tend to appear independently in descendants of the same ancestors.   This is because the descendants must presumably be endowed with somewhat similar potentialities for evolution which they have inherited in common, and they will therefore tend to react in the same way under the influence of similar environmental conditions. Experience has shown, indeed, that as a working hypothesis

it is justifiable to assume that animals which show a pre-
ponderating resemblance to each other anatomically are
genetically related forms, unless some flagrant discrepancy
exists in one or more features such as could only be explained by supposing a long period of independent evolution
from an ancestral form of a much more primitive type.

The Evidence of Fossils

However compelling in the aggregate is all the evidence
for evolution derived from the study of comparative anatomy and embryology, it is of course only indirect evidence.
Much more direct evidence has been collected by biologists
who have actually observed new species arising in nature,
and have also been able to produce them artificially in the
laboratory. But some of the most convincing evidence of
all is provided by the study of fossils (a study which is called
Palaeontology), for this provides the opportunity for examining the actual remains of those intermediate stages which
presumably must have occurred in the evolutionary transformation of one type into another. It has taken a good many
years to collect this evidence, for it is only by a rare chance
that the remains of an animal become sufficiently well
preserved as a fossil in a geological deposit to be of use to a
palaeontologist millions of years after its death. When
Darwin wrote his book on *The Descent of Man* in 1871, there
was almost no fossil evidence in support of his thesis of
human evolution, and many critics seemed to think that
this lack of evidence constituted a most serious objection
to the thesis. To-day, however, the situation is very
different.

As we shall see later, there have now been discovered quite
a number of "missing links" which closely approximate to
just those intermediate stages which had been indirectly
inferred simply by a comparative study of the anatomy and
embryology of living species. Naturally, so far as actual
evidence for evolution is concerned, the most convincing
demonstration is provided by a series of fossils from different
levels in the *same* geological deposits, which show gradual
and progressive modifications in a definite time sequence.
For it is clear that if in the same geographical region large
numbers of fossil remains are found in geological strata of
successive ages, and if they exhibit a graded series of struc-

tural changes linking up an ancient form, X, with a later form, Y, then here we have presumptive evidence of the evolutionary route by which, in the process of time, Y has been derived from X. Some examples of series of this kind are actually available which provide objective evidence of progressive evolutionary change, but, in most cases at present, intermediate stages in the evolutionary development of a particular group of animals are represented by fossils derived from geological deposits in different parts of the world. However, the relative ages of such scattered deposits can usually be satisfactorily established from geological data.

It is well known that the fossil record of evolutionary development is already fairly detailed in the case of some groups of mammals. The pedigree of the horse, for example, is well attested by the remains of extinct forms, starting from *Hyracotherium*, a small creature that lived in Eocene times fifty million years ago or so, and which still had four toes on its fore-foot and three toes on its hind foot, and followed by successive phases in which one toe after another was eliminated until the modern one-toed type of horse appeared. Similarly, stages in the evolutionary history of the elephants can be objectively demonstrated to some extent by reference to the actual remains of ancestral types. There can be little doubt that the continuation of palaeontological research will eventually provide more and more complete series demonstrating in detail the actual evolutionary history of the various other groups of animals which exist to-day. It is for this reason that students of evolution tend to concentrate their attention on the collection and study of fossils.

Fossil remains of extinct Primates are, unfortunately, but rarely come by, for the reason that, being mostly arboreal creatures, they lived in forested regions where the conditions were very unfavourable to the preservation of their remains in a fossilized form. Consequently, the geological history of the Primates has for many years been much less well known than that of some other groups of mammals (for example, horses or elephants). But the fossil evidence is now beginning to accumulate rather rapidly, and there can be no reasonable doubt that in the course of time it will become complete enough to enable us to present the evolutionary history of Man and the other Primates in more detail. Even now, though the palaeontological evidence still remains far from complete, it is already sufficient to justify a sketch in broad outline of the evolutionary path followed by the forerunners of Man.   Indeed, this path can be traced as far back as the time (probably about 70 million years ago) when the earliest Primates made their appearance in this world as quite small and inconspicuous insectivorous mammals living among the branches of the trees. This evidence will be presented as impersonally as possible, with the intention that the reader shall be able to draw his own conclusions.

GEOLOGICAL TIME

Discussions of fossil records can hardly be pursued without a preliminary statement about the time scales used by geologists.   All of the fossils with which we shall be concerned were found in what are called sedimentary deposits, that is to say in geological formations which have been deposited layer by layer under the influence of agents such as running water. Everyone knows that, as it flows rapidly in its upper reaches, a river carries down mud and sand which may be deposited when it slows up towards its mouth. Indeed, some harbours tend to become quite rapidly silted up in this way. Again, it is common knowledge that, in their retreat, floods may leave behind them a thick layer of mud covering everything that has been submerged. The carcase of an animal may become buried by deposits of this sort, and, while the soft parts of the body rapidly rot away, the bones and teeth may be preserved sufficiently long to undergo a permanent mineralization. The mud and sand may in course of time become hardened into shale or sandstone, thus effectively sealing the mineralized remains and keeping them intact for many millions of years. It is obvious that, as sedimentary formations are deposited in this way layer by layer, the more ancient fossils will be found in the deepest layers, and the more recent in the uppermost layers. In just the same sort of way, the remains of cave-living animals may become covered and sealed off by a hard layer of stalagmite (formed by the continual drippings of lime-impregnated water on to the floor of the cave) and, again, the older the fossil, the more deeply will it be found embedded in the stalagmitic floor. It is because of this, of course, that geologists are able to assess the relative antiquity of fossils dug up in the excavation of some particular geological formation. It also enables them to place in their proper chronological order most of the geological formations which make up the crust of the earth, since the later formations normally overlie the earlier, forming a series of layers or strata arranged in regular time sequence. It is unusual in any one locality to find more than a few consecutive formations out of the many which have been deposited in the past, but by comparing one site with another it has been possible finally to arrange them in their correct sequence.

By reference to geological formations, geological time has been subdivided into four main subdivisions or "eras". The oldest and longest of these, which has left few traces of life, is that vast period during which the Pre-Cambrian rocks were formed (see Fig. 1). The succeeding Palaeozoic Era began about 500 million and terminated about 200 million years ago; during the greater part of this era the only vertebrates in existence were fishes of a very primitive type, but towards its end amphibians and reptiles put in an appearance. The Palaeozoic was followed by the Mesozoic Era, which is sometimes called the Age of Reptiles, since it was during this time that the huge dinosaurs, pterodactyls and many other remarkable types of extinct reptile lived and flourished. The Mesozoic Era is further subdivided into three periods, the Triassic, Jurassic and Cretaceous. It was during the last of these that the chalk cliffs in the South of England were deposited as a marine sediment. Towards the end of the Cretaceous period the great reptilian dynasties became extinct, but even before this true mammals had already come into existence. These earliest mammals were small and inconspicuous creatures of exceedingly primitive type. Some of the most ancient groups, whose fossil remains have been found in Jurassic deposits and even in still older Triassic deposits, died out before the end of the Mesozoic Era. But during the Cretaceous period little mammals of more modern type began to flourish, and they included some of the earliest members of the mammalian Orders which exist to-day.

The Mesozoic Era was succeeded, probably about 70 million years ago, by the Caenozoic or Tertiary Era. This is subdivided into the following periods from its commencement: Eocene, Oligocene, Miocene, Pliocene, Pleistocene and Recent.   The relative time intervals occupied by each of these periods is indicated in the accompanying diagram (Fig. 1).   The Pleistocene period, which probably began almost three million years ago, together with the subsequent or Recent period, is sometimes termed the Quaternary, and it is of particular interest since it marks the emergence of *Homo sapiens* and his gradual diffusion over the greater part of the world.   A striking feature of the latter part of the Pleistocene period was the repeated occurrence in many regions of the world of cold periods of the utmost severity—the glaciations of the Ice Age.   The greater part of the British Isles, for example, was on several occasions covered over by ice-sheets formed by the confluence of glaciers which spread down from the regions of high land.   It is now generally agreed that there were four major glaciations, separated by interglacial periods during which the glaciers retreated and the climate became temperate and probably warmer than it is to-day. These startling fluctuations of climate, which were accompanied by large-scale migrations of the Pleistocene fauna (including early Man), were world-wide in their effect, though actual glaciation was confined to an area of the globe extending from the Arctic over the northern part of Europe, Asia and the North American Continent, and from the Antarctic over a corresponding region of the Southern Hemisphere, and to regions surrounding mountain formations, such as the Alps and Himalayas.   Since the several glacial periods can be to some extent equated with each other over different parts of the world, they provide a most useful chronological scale of reference.   The glaciations of the Pleistocene period will be further discussed in the section dealing with the last phases in the evolution of Man (p. 91), but it should be noted here that they were preceded by a lengthy part of the Pleistocene to which the term Villafranchian is applied.

Mention has already been made of the approximate number of years which are estimated to have elapsed since the termination of certain of the main subdivisions of geological time.   The question now arises, how are such estimates arrived at, and how far is it possible to rely on them, even if they are only to be regarded as broad approximations?   The relative lengths of time required for the deposition of some geological formations can be roughly assessed

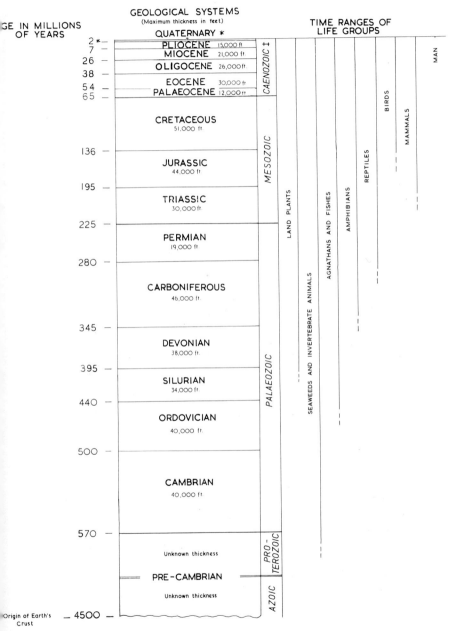

FIG. 1.—Geological Time-scale.

by comparing their relative thicknesses, but, apart from the fact that it involves possible errors of considerable magnitude, this method in any case only provides a relative time scale. There are other methods available for estimating the relative antiquity of fossil remains, and in a number of instances, an *absolute* time scale can also be calculated—a matter of very considerable interest, since this permits a quantitative analysis of the actual rate of evolutionary change. Space does not permit of a discussion here of the different methods whereby attempts have been made to establish relative or absolute chronologies, but information regarding them may be found in some of the literature listed at the end of this book (e.g. *Frameworks for dating Fossil Man*, by K. P. Oakley; and *Human Biology*, by G. A. Harrison and others). It should be mentioned, however, that the time scale and dates to which reference is made in this account are based on estimates of an approximate order only, and certain of them may need revision later. But some of the computations so far completed by various methods are sufficiently consistent to make it probable that they are reasonably correct, at least within broad limits. It is interesting to note that recent reviews of all the fossil evidence, combined with the available geochronological data, lead to the conclusion that it may take as much as 500,000 years for the evolutionary development of a new animal species, and that some modern species are probably at least 30 million years old.

Bones and Teeth

It has already been mentioned in a previous section that the study of fossils, or palaeontology, provides the most direct evidence available for the theory of evolution, since it demonstrates those intermediate or transitional forms which are necessarily postulated by this theory to have existed in past geological ages. It also supplies the objective data from which the actual course of evolution followed by a particular group of animals can be inferred. As a rule, fossils are formed only by the least destructible parts of the body, usually elements of the skeleton, which, under favourable circumstances, are preserved in geological deposits. When an animal dies, the soft parts undergo rapid dissolution, but the bones, since they are composed largely of an inorganic matrix of lime salts, may remain intact for a time. If they chance to be fairly quickly covered up by layers of sediment, such as mud or sand, and thus sealed off and protected from the destructive effects of weathering or from the depredations of carrion eaters, they may become preserved for an indefinite time. Their permanence is usually further ensured by the fact that they become gradually impregnated with mineral salts derived from the deposit in which they lie embedded. Even more resistant to destruction after death are the teeth, for not only are they mainly composed of a durable substance, dentine, which is similar to bony tissue although much denser, they are also capped by an exceedingly hard layer of enamel. Hence it follows that a great deal more is known of the teeth of extinct mammals than of any other part of the body, and for this reason the comparative anatomy and evolution of the dentition have been studied in very considerable detail. Only quite exceptionally are parts of an extinct mammal other than bones and teeth preserved as fossils; examples of these rarities are the remains of a whole mammoth which was found frozen in ice-bound earth in Siberia, and the pieces of dried skin of a giant sloth from a cave in Patagonia.

Although vertebrate palaeontologists deal almost entirely with bones and teeth, they can learn a great deal about the anatomy of the soft parts of an extinct animal simply by studying these remnants. For, in spite of the fact that the dried skeleton of an animal gives an impression of rigidity and permanence, in life bony tissue may be said to be plastic in the sense that during the period of growth it becomes moulded by the soft tissues with which it is in contact. For example, the attachments of muscles are impressed on the limb bones in the form of rough surfaces, ridges and prominences, and some idea of the muscular development can thus be gained by a study of the bones. The soft brain, as it expands in growth, moulds the inside of the bones of the cranium, so that by examining the latter the disposition and complexity of the cerebral convolutions can sometimes be ascertained from their imprints. Nerves and arteries may form grooves where they lie in contact with bones, and thus leave some indication of their size and importance. From his familiarity with matters such as these, the palaeontologist can with little difficulty construct a fairly clear mental picture of the appearance during life of an extinct animal whose skeletal remains he is studying, provided that these remains are sufficiently complete and well preserved, and the evidence which he thus obtains for unravelling the details of evolutionary genealogies is of paramount importance.

It may be thought that, if the reader is not particularly familiar with skeletons and teeth, it will be difficult to present to him in an intelligible form the fossil evidence bearing on the evolution of Man. In fact, the main points of evidence can be made adequately clear as they are put forward, with brief explanatory references where these are necessary. It is convenient, however, to give a little preliminary consideration to certain of the salient features of the skull and teeth, and these can be indicated quite simply in a diagrammatic fashion.

In the accompanying illustration (Fig. 2) are shown in side view the skull of a dog (representing a lower, non-Primate mammal), a chimpanzee and a modern European. Let the reader first give his attention to that part of the skull which contains the brain—the brain-case (sometimes referred to as the *cranium* or *calvaria* to distinguish it from the skull as a whole). Since it fits fairly closely round the brain, its size gives some indication of the degree of cerebral development. In the dog it is much smaller in proportion to the skull as a whole than it is in the chimpanzee, and in the latter it is smaller than in modern Man. The appearance of a progressive increase in the proportionate size of the brain-case is accompanied by a change in its position relative to the facial part of the skull, for whereas in the dog the face is situated mainly in advance of the cranium, in Man it seems by comparison to have become withdrawn below it. This is partly due to the great development of the front part of the brain in Man, which is also responsible for one of his most distinctive features, a more or less vertical forehead. The progressive expansion of the brain leads to certain other changes in the skull. On the top of the dog's skull in the illustration is a median crest of bone projecting up as a sharp flange; this provides an extension of the bony surface which gives attachment to a powerful muscle of mastication attached to the jaw, the temporal muscle. At the back of the skull, also, are prominent bony ridges which serve to

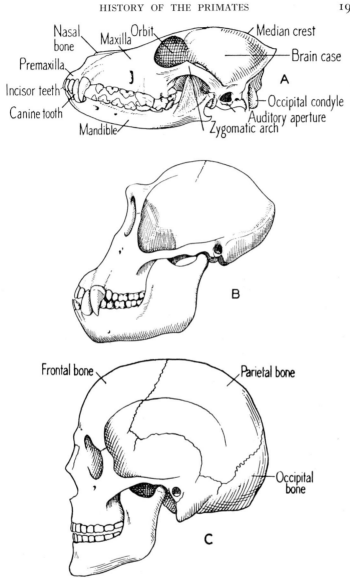

FIG. 2.—The skull of a dog (A), chimpanzee (B) and Man (C) seen from the side, to show the contrast in the relative proportions of the different parts. For the purpose of comparison the skulls are all represented to be of the same length.

attach the muscles of the neck. In many Primates, however, the expansion of the brain-case to a globular form with a relatively more extensive surface provides a sufficient area for the attachment of these muscles without the outgrowth of special crests and flanges.

On either side of the dog's skull in front of the brain-case is seen the bony orbit or eye-socket. In the dog this socket is by no means sharply defined, for it is widely open behind. It is characteristic of the evolution of the Primates that (with the increasing importance of vision and the consequent elaboration of the eye) the orbit becomes quite early surrounded and protected by a complete ring of bone, and later (in monkeys, apes and Man) becomes almost entirely shut off behind by a bony wall. Another developmental trend in the bony orbit which becomes manifested in the evolutionary history of the Primates is related to a shift in the position of the eyes. In most lower mammals the eyes are situated on either side of the head and look outwards. Thus (as in a rabbit, for example) each eye sees quite a different picture. In the higher Primates, on the other hand, the eyes have become rotated so that they look directly forward, and now each eye sees the same field of view (but from a slightly different angle). This new position is essential for what is called "stereoscopic vision", that is, the sort of vision which permits an appreciation of depth and perspective. The acquisition of full stereoscopic vision among mammals is a distinctive character of the higher Primates, and in them the openings of the bony orbits are directed forwards. But even in most of the lower Primates some degree of forward rotation of the eyes has occurred, and this is also reflected in a corresponding shift in the direction of the orbital apertures.

In the cheek region below the orbit is a bony arch, the zygomatic arch, which extends from the aperture of the ear to the upper jaw. This arch bridges over the temporal muscle (already mentioned), and also serves to give attachment to another muscle of mastication, the masseter muscle. Consequently, in lower mammals with powerful jaws and strong masticatory muscles the zygomatic arch is stout and prominent, but in the Primates it tends to become progressively attenuated with the reduction in the relative size of the jaws.

The snout region of the skull is very extensive in the dog, projecting forwards a long way in front of the orbit. It is largely composed of the upper jaw or maxilla, embedded in which are the roots of most of the upper teeth. The front teeth, or incisors, are attached to a separate bony element of the skull called the premaxilla. The lower jaw, or mandible, articulates by a movable joint with the base of the skull just in front of the ear, and contains all the lower teeth. With the dwindling importance of the teeth in the evolution of the Primates (associated with the increasing use of the hands for grasping purposes) the jaws recede, and the effects of this recession are plainly to be seen by comparing the skulls of the dog, chimpanzee and Man shown in Fig. 2. There is another reason why the snout region of the skull undergoes a progressive reduction in the evolution of the Primates. It contains the bony skeleton of the nose, which includes a number of complicated bones covered in life by a delicate membrane sensitive to smells. The apparatus of smell becomes much less important for the arboreal life of Primates as compared with lower mammals of terrestrial habitat. Consequently it dwindles in size and complexity, and with it the snout region as a whole becomes less prominent.

One more feature of the skull deserves attention here. It is the large opening, called the foramen magnum, through which the spinal cord passes to become continuous with the brain, and alongside which are the occipital condyles by which the whole skull articulates with the neck region of the backbone (Fig. 3). In four-footed animals such as the dog the foramen magnum is situated at the back of the skull, for in these animals the backbone in the standing position is usually held more or less horizontally, and the skull projects forwards from its front end. In Man the backbone is normally held vertically, with the skull balanced on its upper end, and, in relation to this different type of posture, the foramen magnum is on the under surface of the skull, facing downwards. In most living Primates the foramen is to some degree displaced from the back of the skull towards its under-surface, but the extent of this displacement varies, becoming in general greater as we pass up the scale from lemurs, through monkeys and apes, to Man himself. It will be realized that by noting the position of the foramen magnum in a fossil skull we can get important

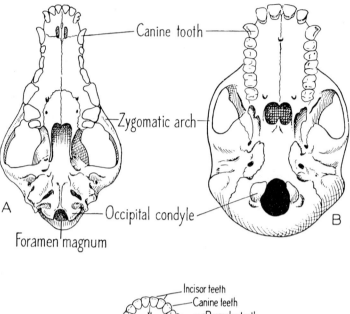

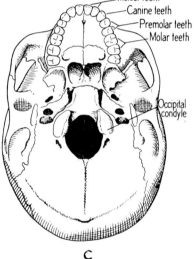

Fig. 3.—The basal aspect of the skull of a dog (A), chimpanzee
(B) and Man (C) with the lower jaw removed. The foramen
magnum, which is placed at the back end of the skull in the
dog, is situated relatively further forward in the chimpanzee,
and much more so in Man. Note also that the relative length
of the palate diminishes in this series.

information about the poise of the head during life, and also about the posture of the animal as a whole.

We may now summarize briefly the main trends in the evolution of the Primates so far as they have been manifested in the skull (see Fig. 13). These trends are as follows: (1) The progressive enlargement of the brain case or cranium, which becomes more globular in shape and often lacks the prominent bony crests or flanges found in many lower mammals. (2) The enclosure of the orbit by a complete bony ring and, in higher Primates, the formation of a bony wall shutting it off behind. (3) The gradual rotation forwards of the orbits until their openings look directly forwards. (4) The attenuation of the bony arch of the cheek (zygomatic arch). (5) The recession of the snout, and the retraction of the face to a position below rather than in front of the cranium. (6) The shrinkage of the bony apparatus of the nose. (7) The progressive shifting of the foramen magnum from the back end of the skull to its basal surface, so that it comes to face downwards instead of more or less directly backwards.

The main features of the mammalian dentition and the evolution of the teeth in the Primates may be summarized as follows: In typical mammals the dentition is made up of teeth of various types. If the reader will examine his own dentition he will find that in front of the jaws on either side are two teeth of spatulate form with a fairly straight, chisel-like, cutting edge (see Fig. 3C). These are the *incisor teeth*, and their main function is to bite off pieces of food which are then transferred back for the attention of the grinding teeth behind. Behind the incisor teeth is the somewhat pointed *canine tooth* (or "eye tooth"), whose prominence varies considerably from one individual to another. In many mammals it is used for grasping prey and as a weapon in attack and defence. Behind the canine tooth are two *premolar teeth* (or bicuspids)—teeth of relatively simple construction, in each of which the crown is raised into two little eminences or cusps, one to the inner and one to the outer side. Behind the premolar teeth are three *molar* or grinding teeth, the crowns of which have a more complicated pattern of four or five cusps. The molars are used for crushing food and chewing it up into small fragments.

In mammals generally these four categories of teeth can be distinguished, though the number and shape of the teeth show considerable variation. Their number is commonly expressed, for brevity, by a simple formula. The dental formula for Man is $\frac{2.1.2.3}{2.1.2.3} \times 2 = 32$, which means that in the upper and lower jaws there are normally on either side two incisors, one canine, two premolars and three molars, or thirty-two teeth in all. Incidentally, it may be noted that all these teeth of the adult dentition are preceded in babyhood by temporary or "milk" teeth, with the exception of the molars, which have no temporary precursors.

When true mammals first appeared, they seem to have experimented with different kinds of molar teeth. Some developed teeth adapted for crushing food, with highly complicated crowns beset with a large number of small tubercles. Other mammals developed sharp, shearing molars, the teeth of the upper jaw working against those of the lower jaw like the blades of a pair of scissors. In the ancestors of all the modern mammals (apart from the egg-laying mammals of Australasia) the molar teeth acquired crowns of triangular shape, with a sharp tubercle or cusp at each corner of the triangle. This kind of molar tooth—the *tri-tubercular* or *tribosphenic* pattern—proved exceptionally efficient, since it combined in one tooth the several functions of grasping, shearing, and crushing or chewing. It was from these simple tritubercular molar teeth that the variously complicated molar teeth of all placental mammals (including the Primates) were eventually developed by a process of gradual evolutionary change.

Now let us consider the nature of the dentition of the common ancestral stock of mammals which gave rise to the different existing orders of placental mammals,* including the Primates. It seems certain—on the evidence of comparative anatomy and the fossil record—that in its general features it must have approximated very closely to the arrangement shown in Fig. 4. The dental formula was $\frac{3.1.4.3}{3.1.4.3} \times 2 = 44$; this represents the full complement of teeth in a completely generalized placental mammal, from

* Placental mammals include all existing mammals except the egg-laying mammals (monotremes) and the marsupials.

which the different formulae found in most living placental mammals have been derived by some degree of reduction. The incisor teeth in the ancestral stock were probably small and cylindrical, with rounded tips. The canine was a conical tooth, with a pointed tip projecting beyond the level of the neighbouring teeth. The premolar teeth were each of simple form with a single pointed cusp. The molars must all have shown the primitive tritubercular pattern of cusps.

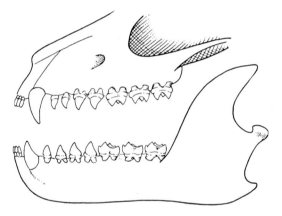

FIG. 4.—A diagram showing the probable appearance of the dentition of the ancestral mammalian stock from which all placental mammals have been derived in the course of evolution. In each jaw are seen three small incisor teeth in front, a sharp projecting canine tooth, four premolar teeth of a simple construction, and three molar teeth.

We must now briefly consider the general developmental tendencies shown in the evolution of the dentition in Primates. The fossil evidence shows that very early in their evolutionary history most of the Primates lost one incisor on each side of the upper and lower jaws, and, indeed, the possession of two incisors (instead of the original three) is often cited as one of the distinctive characters of the existing Primates. But in some lemurs the reduction has gone further, for in certain species the upper incisors have almost disappeared. In the higher Primates, the Anthropoidea (monkeys, apes and Man), the incisors have lost their peg-like character and have taken on a spatulate form with a fairly straight cutting edge. Finally, we should note that, with one exception, in all the modern lemurs the lower incisors, together with the lower canine teeth, have become elongated into slender points and are close-set like the teeth of a fine comb. Indeed, they are actually used by their owners for combing their fur, and form what is sometimes called a "dental comb" (Fig. 5).

The canine teeth in many Primates became enlarged to form sharp and powerful dagger-like teeth (for example, in the larger monkeys, such as baboons). On the other hand, in their size and shape they have in some instances become approximated to the incisors and almost indistinguishable from them.

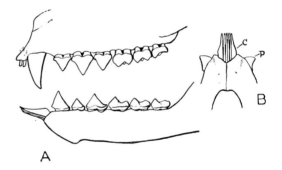

Fig. 5.—The dentition of *Lemur*, natural size. In the side view (A) the upper incisor teeth are seen to be much reduced, while the canine tooth is sharp and dagger-like. Behind the canine are three premolars and three molars. In the lower jaw the incisor teeth and the canine project forwards and form the "dental comb". The latter is shown to better effect from below in (B). Since the canine (c) takes part in this curious modification, the front premolar tooth (p) has secondarily assumed the functions of a canine tooth, and has become sharp and pointed.

The premolars in the early stages of Primate evolution showed a tendency, in the first place, to a diminution in size of the first two and a relative enlargement of the third and fourth, and subsequently to a disappearance of the first premolar, and later (as seen in Old World monkeys,

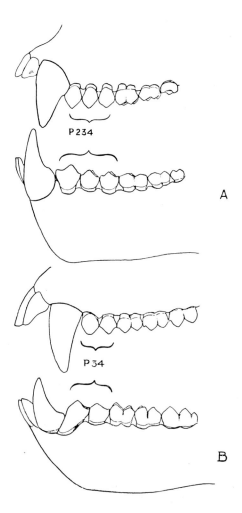

FIG. 6.—The dentition of (A) a New World monkey (*Cebus*) and (B) an Old World monkey (*Macaca*), natural size. As in all modern Primates there are only two incisor teeth in each jaw in both cases. In the New World monkeys the first premolar tooth of the ancestral mammalian stock has been lost, leaving only three. In the Old World monkeys the second premolar tooth has also disappeared, so that in these Primates (as also in the anthropoid apes and Man) the dental formula is 2 . 1 . 2 . 3.

apes and Man) of the second premolars also (Fig. 6). Moreover, the third and fourth premolars quite early became
complicated by the appearance of a second cusp, so that
they came to assume a "bicuspid" character, and in some
cases they became even more complicated.

The prevailing trend in the evolution of the molar teeth
in the Primates has been manifested in a tendency to trans-
form their primitive trituberclar pattern into a quadritubercular, or 4-cusped, form. The gradual conversion of
the primitive trituberclar molars into quadritubercular
teeth is well attested by the fossil evidence, for all stages of
this slow evolutionary process can be recognized in the teeth
of the extinct early Primates.

THE PRIMATES AS THEY ARE TO-DAY

As we have already seen, Man belongs (zoologically speaking) to the Order Primates. This implies that, in common
with the other representatives of the Order, he belongs to a
natural group whose members have become gradually di-
versified during the course of evolution from a common
ancestral stock. Thus, in order to appreciate fully the
evolutionary history of the human species, it is necessary
also to make some reference to that of the Order to which
he belongs. Only by so doing will it become clear just how
Man stands in relation to the animal kingdom as a whole.
But, before discussing the fossil evidence for their evolutionary history, it is first desirable to give a brief account of the
various subdivisions of the Primates as they exist to-day;
that is to say, as they are represented by all those terminal
products of evolution which still survive.

It is peculiarly difficult to give a satisfying definition of
the Primates, since there is no single distinguishing feature
which characterizes all the members of the group. While
many other mammalian Orders can be defined by conspicuous specializations of a positive kind which readily
mark them off from one another, the Primates as a whole
have preserved rather a generalized anatomy and, if anything, are to be mainly distinguished from other Orders by
a negative feature—their *lack* of specialization. Thus they
have mostly maintained a generalized structure of their
limbs, preserving the primitive pentadactyly (i.e. five fingers
and five toes), as well, also, as keeping intact certain elements

of the limb skeleton (such as the clavicle or collar-bone) which tend to shrink or disappear in some other groups of mammals. Again, the grinding teeth (or molars) preserve, on the whole, a simple and primitive structure, particularly when compared with the complicated and highly specialized teeth which have been developed in some Orders (such as the elephants, ungulates and carnivores).

It has been pointed out and emphasized by many comparative anatomists that the relative lack of specialization shown among the Primates is consequent upon the circumstances of their particular habitat for, with only a few exceptions, all the Primates are arboreal creatures and live in tropical or sub-tropical regions. Now there is considerable reason to believe that the prototype of mammals as a whole was arboreal in its way of life. As far as the limbs are concerned, this sort of life necessarily requires those grasping functions which are clearly dependent on primitive features, such as pentadactyly, with a wide range of movement of the fingers and toes, a well-developed clavicle (which is used as a strut for sideways movements of the arms) and so forth. Therefore, since from the outset of their evolutionary origin from the arboreal mammalian prototype the Primates remained in the trees, they tended to preserve these advantageous, though primitive, anatomical characters. In many other matters, also, an arboreal habitat favours the preservation of a generalized kind of bodily structure. As far as the dentition is concerned, an arboreal kind of life obviates the necessity for developing highly specialized grinding teeth, since the diet available to most tree-living mammals in the tropics, consisting of leaves, shoots, soft fruits and insects, can be adequately masticated by molar teeth of relatively simple structure.

On the other hand, the early mammals which descended from the trees to enter on terrestrial careers developed all sorts of specializations quite rapidly. For example, their limbs tended to lose their grasping functions, and to become adapted simply as supporting struts for the body or as instruments of high speed, and so they lost one or more toes and other elements such as the clavicle. Their molars in many cases tended to become exceedingly complicated grinding mechanisms in order to deal efficiently with hard roots or tough grass (as in the herbivores), or they became modified to form sharp shears for cutting flesh (as in the carnivores). Many of them developed large horns, fierce tusks, sharp spines, powerful claws, and other weapons of attack and defence, such as are not appropriate in an arboreal life where agility, cunning, and the protection of foliage offer far better prospects of security and survival. The demand for skill and cunning in arboreal life was, no doubt, one of the reasons why the brain began to expand in size and complexity very early in the evolutionary history of the Primates.

Another feature of terrestrial life is the encouragement it gives to the development of a highly specialized smelling, or olfactory, apparatus. For following the scent in tracking prey, or for detecting the proximity of enemies, the sense of smell is far more valuable on the ground than in the trees. On the other hand, life in the trees favours the development of good eyesight for several reasons, particularly for the accurate judging of distance and direction in arboreal acrobatics. Thus in terrestrial mammals the olfactory organs tend to become larger and more elaborate, while at the same time the apparatus of vision often remains rather poorly developed. In the arboreal Primates, on the other hand, the converse tendencies are shown, for in the course of evolution the visual organs become more elaborate and more perfectly adapted to the needs of their environment, while the olfactory apparatus actually dwindles in size and complexity. Incidentally, also, the grasping functions of the hand and foot are further enhanced in most Primates by the transformation of sharp claws (characteristic of primitive mammals) into flattened nails. The latter are associated with the development of highly sensitive pads at the tips of the digits, which provide a very efficient grasping mechanism capable of quite delicate manipulations. One more point which we may note here is that in the evolution of the Primates the grasping pentadactyl hands become more and more used for functions which in four-footed terrestrial mammals are often performed by the front teeth (incisors and canines); consequently, the jaws and teeth tend to become much smaller and less obtrusive.

It has already been mentioned that one of the features common to the Primates is the use of the limbs for grasping purposes. Now there are good grounds for inferring that, even in the primitive mammalian stock from which the earliest Primates had their evolutionary origin, the hand and foot were capable of some degree of prehension, in the sense that the five digits could be splayed out and bent together in a converging movement so as to permit the grasping of small objects. This "flexion-convergence" movement has become considerably amplified in the Primates, particularly in the case of the thumb and big toe which have tended to increase their relative size and to become capable of being moved in opposition to the other digits for grasping purposes. This "opposability" of the thumb and big toe is characteristic of most of the living Primates, so that the foot as well as the hand has a "hand-like" appearance. It is for this reason that the old naturalists in the middle of the last century gave the name "Quadrumana" to the whole group of monkeys and apes, thus distinguishing them from the "Bimana," which included Man.

In the preceding paragraphs we have noted some of the evolutionary tendencies manifested by the Primates in response to the demands of their arboreal environment. Of course, they have not all been realized to anything like the same degree, even by the various members of the Order which exist to-day, and it is for this reason that it is not possible to define the Primates by any one distinguishing feature. The problem of definition becomes more difficult still if we take into account the fossil Primates, particularly the most ancient forms which were just beginning to become differentiated from the generalized mammalian stock that also gave rise to other Orders, and in which, therefore, many of the characteristic Primate features had hardly had time to manifest themselves. Broadly speaking, however, it is now possible to define the Primates on the basis of the prevailing tendencies which dominated their evolutionary development. Using such criteria we may say that they form a natural group of mammals distinguished from other groups by the following prevailing evolutionary tendencies: the preservation of a generalized structure in the limbs, associated with free mobility of the digits (especially the thumb and big toe) and the replacement of sharp compressed claws by flattened nails, the elaboration of their visual powers and a corresponding reduction of the olfactory apparatus, the shortening of the snout or muzzle, the preservation of a relatively simple pattern of molar teeth, and the progressive development of large and complicated brains. In Man some of these tendencies (particularly the expansion of the brain) have advanced much further than in other Primates, and he shows a unique specialization in his "hind limbs", for these have now become transformed into "lower limbs" for supporting the rest of the body in the erect position, while the mobility of the foot and toes (so characteristic of the Primates in general) has become secondarily lost.

Various methods of classification have from time to time been suggested by comparative anatomists and palaeontologists for splitting up the Order of the Primates into the natural subdivisions which most accurately reflect their true genetic inter-relationships. As a matter of convenience we shall follow here the authoritative and generally accepted scheme of classification put forward by Dr. G. G. Simpson. According to this classification, the Primates are divided into two sub-Orders, the Prosimii and the Anthropoidea. The latter includes Man, anthropoid apes and monkeys, and the former the tarsiers, lemurs and tree-shrews.

The members of the Anthropoidea, as this name implies, are distinguished by their rather man-like appearance, an appearance which catches the attention of the most unsophisticated eye. The human resemblance of the apes and monkeys resolves itself on analysis into a few outstanding characters, such as the relatively voluminous and rounded brain-case, the flatness of the face, the position of the eyes (which look directly forward and so appear rather close-set), the shrunken appearance of the ears (which do not stand out from the head as in most lower mammals), the alertness and versatility of the facial expression, the mobility of the lips (and especially the upper lip, which is not bound down to the gums in front as in most lower mammals), the employment for grasping purposes of what is obviously a real "hand" (and not a fore-foot), and the presence of flattened nails on the digits of the hand and foot. These superficial human resemblances of the sub-human members of the Anthropoidea are paralleled by many remarkable features of an even more fundamental character, such as are shown in the reproductive functions, the physiology of the brain, or the microscopic structure of certain organs of the body.

The Anthropoidea are further subdivided into three super-families, Hominoidea (including Man and the anthropoid apes), Cercopithecoidea (Old World monkeys), and Ceboidea (New World monkeys). The grouping together, in the one category Hominoidea, of Man and anthropoid apes is an indication of the close resemblances which they show in their anatomical structure. This group is subdivided into two families, the *Hominidae*, which includes modern and extinct forms of Man, and the *Pongidae*, which includes the modern and extinct anthropoid apes.

Anthropoid Apes

The living anthropoid apes approximate more nearly to Man than do the monkeys in a number of significant features, including the configuration and relative size of the brain, many details of the skull, skeleton and dentition, the tendency towards the adoption of an erect or "orthograde" posture of the trunk (which is correlated with certain features such as the shape of the chest and the disposition of the abdominal organs), the absence of a tail, and so forth. But, apart from structural similarities, they show some remarkable affinities to Man in many of their fundamental physiological processes—for example, the chemical reactions of their blood, the pattern of their growth, certain aspects of the physiology of the brain, the structural details of the tissues through which the young are nourished in the womb before birth, and even the kind of parasitic infestation to which they are susceptible.

All this sort of evidence indicates a relatively close genetic relationship, even though it seems certain that some of the less fundamental resemblances are at least partly to be ascribed to the results of parallel evolution. It must also be emphasized that all the anthropoid apes which exist to-day, in adaptation to their particular arboreal habits of life, have undergone a considerable amount of divergent specialization peculiar to themselves. Thus the mode of progression among the trees by swinging from bough to bough with their arms (brachiation) has led to a great lengthening of the arms, to a relative shrinkage of the thumb (the hand becoming modified functionally to form a sort of "hook" rather than a grasping mechanism, so as to allow of a very rapid release in swinging among the trees), and to an evolutionary dwindling of the hind-limbs. It is to be noted, however, that the gorilla and chimpanzee have secondarily acquired more terrestrial habits and do not "brachiate" freely like the gibbon and orang utan, but they do show, in the construction of the limbs, the same adaptive specializations that are related to a more exclusively arboreal life. We shall refer to such aberrant developments later in discussing the derivation of Man from

Wilson

FIG. 7.—Gorilla.

an ape-like ancestor, but it may be pointed out now that these arboreal specializations have been avoided in Man—in other words, *in these particular respects* Man himself is actually more primitive and generalized than the modern anthropoid apes. As we shall see, also, in some of the extinct types of anthropoid ape it is important to note that the limbs had not yet developed the aberrant specializations characteristic of the modern apes.

Apart from quite a number of extinct forms, the anthropoid apes are represented by only four living types, the Gorilla, Chimpanzee, Orang Utan and Gibbon. The gorilla inhabits the equatorial regions of Africa and is the largest of the living anthropoid apes. Although to-day it is only slightly arboreal, spending most of its life moving about in the undergrowth of the jungle and usually adopting a quadrupedal gait (Fig. 7), the anatomical evidence indicates clearly that the gorilla has only recently in its evolutionary history abandoned brachiating habits, and, in association with the latter, its limbs had evidently become modified in the same way as in the other apes. Closely related to the gorilla is the chimpanzee, which has a similar but rather more extended habitat in tropical Africa, and is smaller and a much more active climber. The orang utan is an Asiatic ape confined to-day to Borneo and Sumatra, but in past geological times it extended its range as far north as China. It attains to a fairly large size and is exclusively arboreal, descending but rarely to the ground. These three apes may be referred to as the giant anthropoid apes, in contrast to the gibbon, which is a relatively much smaller animal. Gibbons are found in the south-eastern parts of Asia, extending over a fairly wide area in Malaya. They are somewhat slenderly built, extremely agile, and their arms attain to a great length (Frontispiece, E). They are the most vocal of the anthropoid apes and roam through the forests in family groups of which several may occupy adjacent or overlapping territories. Another point of particular interest about the gibbon is that it is much more adept at bipedal progression than the larger apes. Indeed, it can run with considerable speed in the erect position, not only along the boughs of trees, but also on the ground, all the time holding out its long arms as balancers. But this bipedal gait is to be regarded as exceptional, for, in the wild, gibbons normally travel among the branches by swinging arm over arm in a suspended position and only very rarely descend to the ground.

MONKEYS

The monkeys represent the lowest stratum of the Anthropoidea which exist to-day. Most of them are thoroughly arboreal, but many (especially some of the Old World monkeys) quite frequently come to the ground, and some are wholly terrestrial. Both among the branches and on the ground they commonly assume a quadrupedal (or pronograde) posture and gait.   They are not such specialized arboreal acrobats as the anthropoid apes, for they move about rather by running and leaping among the larger boughs than by swinging along in brachiating fashion. Hence in most cases they have avoided the disproportionate lengthening of the arms characteristic of the anthropoid apes, and have preserved the more primitive proportions of the limbs—that is to say, the fore-limbs are commonly not much longer than the hind-limbs and may even be shorter. The majority, also, have well-developed tails. The monkeys are divided into

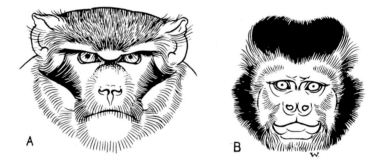

Fig. 8.—(A) An Old World or Catarrhine monkey (*Macaca*) and (B) a New World or Platyrrhine monkey (*Cebus*), showing the difference in the disposition of the nostrils.

two clearly defined groups, the Old World or "Catarrhine" monkeys and the New World or "Platyrrhine" monkeys. The significance of these terms is related to the disposition of the nostrils, though this is a distinction which is not always very striking (Fig. 8).   In the Catarrhine monkeys the nostrils are separated by a relatively narrow partition, whereas in the Platyrrhine monkeys the partition is relatively broad, so that the nostrils are rather wide apart.   These two groups of monkeys are not only sharply contrasted in their geographical distribution, they are also to be distinguished by many important anatomical characters (for example, in the dentition and the structure of the skull). In Dr. Simpson's classification they form two separate super-families, the Cercopithecoidea (Old World monkeys) and the Ceboidea (New World monkeys).

The Old World monkeys comprise one family only, the *Cercopithecidae*, and they have a wide distribution over Asia and Africa, even reaching into Southern Europe. One of the commonest kinds of these monkeys are the macaques; there are about fifty different species, and their geographical range extends from Gibraltar and North Africa in the West (where they are represented by the so-called Barbary Ape), through India, Burma, Malaya, Siam and China, to Japan in the East. All the macaque monkeys are rather stoutly built animals of moderate size and, being exceptionally hardy, can accustom themselves to many different climates, from tropical jungle to the snow-covered heights of mountains. It is because of their hardiness that macaque monkeys were so commonly used for exhibition at country fairs or in small travelling zoos. Another group of Old World monkeys comprises the mangabeys. These are restricted to Africa, and are characterized by rather long tails and by conspicuous white marks on the eyebrows and upper eyelids. They are more thoroughly arboreal than the macaques, and more slender in build. The guenons are a large group of monkeys, also confined in their geographical distribution to Africa. They comprise a considerable number of species, many of which are variously coloured with rather unusual tints. In this character, however, they are surpassed by the guereza monkeys, in which the development of long parti-coloured "manes" of hair on either side of the body is a striking feature. Having adopted a purely arboreal life, the guerezas have gone even further than the anthropoid apes in the reduction of the thumb, for this digit has been reduced to a mere nodule at the side of the hand.

The langurs are Asiatic monkeys, extending from India and Ceylon through Malaya to Tibet and Java. They are mostly of rather large size, but they are lightly built. They feed mainly on leaves and the young shoots of certain plants and, in association with their special vegetarian habits, they have developed large and unusually complicated stomachs. Allied to the langurs is the remarkable proboscis monkey, which to-day is only found in Borneo. It is a grotesque

FIG. 9.—Olive Baboon (*Choeropithecus anubis*).

FIG. 10.—Female Brown Capuchin Monkey (*Cebus*).

looking animal, for it has developed a fleshy nose or proboscis which, in the male, is about three inches long, and projects forwards in a dependent fashion over the mouth. The significance of this proboscis is not clear, for it is not related to an accentuation of the sense of smell. Since it is very much reduced in the female, it can only be inferred that it is a sexual character—that is to say, an adornment for the male.

Lastly, we may refer to certain terrestrial representatives of the Old World monkeys, the baboons and mandrills. These inhabit rocky, open country, and seem to have abandoned arboreal habits almost entirely. They are quadrupedal animals of formidable appearance (Fig. 9), with large projecting muzzles and tails of moderate length, and they usually live in well-established communities.

The New World or Platyrrhine monkeys (Ceboidea) are to-day confined to South America, and comprise a large number of different genera which vary considerably in size and appearance. They are thoroughly arboreal in their habits, and many of them (in contrast with the Old World monkeys) have developed prehensile tails by means of which they can hang and swing from the branches, or which they can even use as a "third hand" for grasping objects, such as food. It has been suggested that this additional arboreal adaptation is related to the fact that in large areas of the tropical forests of South America the ground is swampy or actually under water—thus the monkeys are compelled to become much more completely specialized for a life spent entirely in the trees. Arboreal specialization is carried to its extreme by the spider monkey, in which the prehensile tail is provided with a naked sensory surface on its under aspect near its tip. These animals have also developed arms of inordinate length and, with the use of the hand mainly as a sort of hook for suspension from the branches, the thumb has shrivelled to a small excrescence, or has practically disappeared altogether. One of the commoner kinds of New World monkey is the capuchin monkey, a rather small animal which is a familiar inhabitant of most zoological gardens, and, since it is naturally of a gentle disposition and rather attractive in appearance, is sometimes kept as a pet. The capuchin monkeys are so called because they often show a conspicuous crest of hair on the top of the head, in which a fanciful resemblance to the monk's cowl

may be seen (Fig. 10). Another attractive genus is represented by the squirrel monkey, an animal about the size of
the ordinary squirrel and distinguished by having a brain
which appears *relatively* rather large. Much bigger animals
are the Saki monkeys, characterized by the length of their
tails (which, in this case, are not prehensile), and the Uakari
monkeys in which the tail has actually undergone some reduction. The night monkeys, or Douroucoulis, are unique
among all monkeys because of their nocturnal habits. In
association with these habits the eyes are large, and the
structure of the retina is also adapted for night vision.

Fig. 11.—Common Marmoset (*Callithrix*).

The largest of the New World monkeys are the Howlers,
so called because of their well-developed vocal powers. The
hyoid bone (embedded in the base of the tongue) is curiously
modified in these animals to form a sort of resonating
chamber in the throat, whereby the volume of sound emitted
is much amplified. Lastly, we may mention the little marmosets, the smallest of all living monkeys, and also in many
respects the most primitive (Fig. 11). They are contrasted

with the other New World monkeys not only in their size, but by the fact that they have only two (instead of three) molar teeth on each side of the jaw, and (except for the great toe) all the digits are furnished with sharp curved claws instead of flattened nails.

Tarsiers

It has already been mentioned that the sub-order of the Primates called Prosimii includes tarsiers, lemurs and tree-shrews. The first of these comprise a group of small Primates which, from the anatomical point of view, seem in several respects to occupy a position intermediate between the apes and monkeys on the one hand, and the lemurs on the other. Some authorities have suggested that since they are so much more "advanced" than lemurs in their anatomy they should really be regarded as primitive monkeys, but, in fact, they are in many ways much inferior to a simian status. In past geological times tarsiers were very wide-spread over most parts of the world, and reached a con-siderable diversity in their anatomical structure. To-day they are represented by one genus only, *Tarsius*, a little animal which is found in Borneo, the Philippines, and the Celebes (Frontispiece, c). This surviving tarsier is only the size of a two-weeks-old kitten, and has attracted consider-able attention partly because of its bizarre appearance, and partly because it combines in its anatomy a number of remarkably primitive with unexpectedly advanced charac-ters. The tarsier is a nocturnal and entirely arboreal creature, and is mainly insectivorous. It exhibits a marked degree of specialization in the enormous size of its eyes and in the peculiar modification of its hind-limbs which allow it to make powerful jumps in leaping about from branch to branch. It can jump a distance of six feet with consider-able accuracy. The ears are large, and the tail (which is not prehensile in the usual sense of the term) is long and naked except for a terminal tuft of hair. In the structure of its nose and lips the tarsier resembles the monkeys and contrasts rather strongly with the lemurs. Other features in which it approximates to the monkeys include the structure of the brain (especially that part concerned with vision), the internal anatomy of the nose and the details of the reproductive apparatus.

LEMURS

The members of this group of Primates display their Primate status much less obtrusively than the monkeys, and in many respects they appear to represent a midway stage between monkeys and lower non-Primate mammals. It is for this reason that they are sometimes (with the tarsiers) referred to as prosimians, while German naturalists have always termed them "Halbaffen" or half-apes. Their kinship with the higher Primates is indicated by the evolutionary tendencies which they have shown in the past, and by a number of anatomical features such as the structure of the brain, the functional adaptation of the limbs for grasping purposes, the freedom and mobility of the thumb and big toe (leading to the appearance of a "hand" rather than a "paw"), and the presence of flattened nails on the digits.* On the other hand, a strong contrast to the monkeys (and a corresponding approximation to non-Primate mammals) is provided by the elongated snout, which projects forwards well beyond the level of the chin, the naked and moist area of skin around the nostrils, the median cleft in the upper lip where the latter is bound down to the underlying gum, the large and mobile ears, and the relatively immobile expression of the face. The lemurs are almost all entirely arboreal creatures; many are also nocturnal in their activities and this is reflected in the rather large size of their eyes. They are divided into two separate groups, and though on superficial inspection these may not show marked differences, they are strongly contrasted in a number of apparently fundamental features, such as the structure of the skull. The two groups are officially termed the Lemuriformes and the Lorisiformes. The former are sometimes called the true lemurs, and to-day they are entirely confined to Madagascar and some small neighbouring islands. They vary considerably in size, and the best known species to be seen in zoological gardens are the brown lemur and the ring-tailed lemur (Fig. 12). About the size of cats, and equally docile, these animals are good climbers, using their long furry tails as a sort of balancing apparatus. The smallest of the Madagascar lemurs is the mouse lemur, a fluffy little

---

* An elongated claw is, however, always retained on the second toe. This toe is thus used for scratching purposes, and is sometimes called the "toilet digit".

animal of very attractive appearance. The most curious species is the Aye-Aye (*Daubentonia*). This peculiar lemur is characterized by the possession of large chisel-like front teeth, which are used for gnawing and somewhat resemble the incisor teeth of rodents. It is also distinguished by the retention of sharp, curved claws on all its digits, with the only exception of the big toe which is furnished with a flat nail. So remarkable is the Aye-Aye that some authorities have urged its separation from other lemurs as a distinct sub-Order of the Primates.

Wilson.

FIG. 12.—Ring-tailed Lemurs (*Lemur catta*).

The Lorisiformes include all those lemurs which are found on the mainland of Africa (e.g. the galagos, pottos and awantibos) and in Asia (the lorises). The latter are extremely slow-moving creatures, climbing about among the branches with a very deliberate, almost crawling, gait. They have relatively large eyes, and the snout is a good deal shorter than in most of the true lemurs. The galagos, or "bush-babies", are rather small animals and, like the tarsier, their hind-limbs have become specially modified for jumping purposes (Frontispiece, B).

TREE-SHREWS

Now we come to the most lowly members of the Primates—the tree-shrews (Frontispiece, A). Indeed, so lowly are they and so unlike other Primates in their superficial characters, that until recently they were classified with the Insectivora (which include hedgehogs, ground-shrews and so forth). Some zoologists even now are in some doubt whether they should be promoted to the Primates, for they differ quite obviously in a number of seemingly important characters. In many ways, also, they are remarkably primitive animals. Indeed, it seems very probable that the tree-shrews represent in their general structure a tolerably close approximation to the earliest phases in the evolution of the Primates from generalized mammalian ancestors. Hence it is important that the reader should have a fairly clear idea of their appearance (though, unfortunately, they are but rarely seen in zoological gardens).

The living tree-shrews have a wide distribution in southeast Asia, extending over India, Burma, the Malay Peninsula, Sumatra, Java and Borneo, and are represented by a number of species. The smaller species are very active arboreal mammals, living mainly among the higher branches of the trees, while the larger species are rather to be regarded as bush animals, inhabiting the lower branches of the trees and the undergrowth of the forest. They all have quite a close superficial resemblance to squirrels; indeed the zoological name for the superfamily which includes them, Tupaioidea, is derived from the Malay word "tupai" which means a squirrel. The resemblance is enhanced by the long and bushy tails which many of them possess. In size the tree-shrews vary much as the different kinds of squirrel do, and like some of the oriental squirrels they may be quite strikingly coloured, with vivid shoulder stripes and other markings. They differ from squirrels in having rather more pointed muzzles and smaller ears (which are curiously human in the details of their shape), and in the greater mobility of the "fingers" and "toes." These digits, particularly those which are equivalent to the big toe and thumb, are capable of a considerable range of movement, and can be effectively used for grasping purposes. In these functions can be seen the initial stages which led to the development of the prehensility so characteristic of the "quadrumanous" extremities of the higher Primates. All the digits are furnished with sharp curved claws, and herein the tree-shrews stand in rather marked contrast to the Primates as a whole, but we have already noted that even in the marmosets most of the digits are clawed. Thus, in the definition of the Primates, the distinction between claws and nails is not so fundamental as might appear on first sight. Another feature in which the tree-shrews are quite different from squirrels is the character of the front teeth, for while squirrels have the

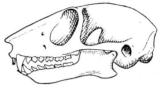

A
B

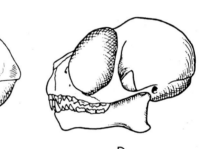

C
D

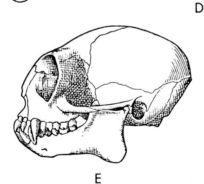

E

FIG. 13.—The skulls of some lower Primates, somewhat greater than natural size. (A) Tree-shrew (*Ptilocercus*). (B) Mouse lemur (*Microcebus*). (C) An Eocene Tarsioid (*Necrolemur*). (D) The modern Tarsier (*Tarsius*). (E) Marmoset (*Callithrix*). Note the increase in the relative size of the brain-case and the recession of the snout and jaws in this graded series connecting the tree-shrew with the monkey.

chisel-like gnawing incisor teeth distinctive of all rodents, in the tree-shrews the incisors are of a relatively simple type. The lower incisors are styliform and strongly procumbent, and it is interesting to note that they are used as a "dental comb" for the toilet of the fur as in the lemurs (see p. 26). The tree-shrews are predominantly insectivorous in their diet, feeding on cicadas, flies, grasshoppers, cockroaches and so forth. They have also been reported on occasion to eat fruit and seeds, and even mice.

Almost all the tree-shrews are diurnal animals and, associated with their agility and quick movements, they have a particularly alert expression which seems to be accentuated by their relatively large eyes.

Now, as we have already noted (p.20), one of the outstanding features in the evolution of the Primates is the progressive elaboration of the sense of vision, which is reflected not only in the perfection of the structural mechanism of the eye itself, but also in the development and expansion of the visual centres in the brain. This tendency is already manifest in the tree-shrews; herein they show a striking approach to the lemurs, and a corresponding divergence from the true insectivores with which in the past they have usually been associated by zoologists. The superficial appearance of the living tree-shrews gives no indication that the brain is conspicuous for its size, yet, compared with the true insectivores, it shows quite a definite expansion of that part which is related to the more complex cerebral functions (that is to say, the cerebral cortex), particularly those areas concerned with vision. On the other hand, the smell apparatus of the brain shows some signs of retrogression, and here, again, is another indication that they have to some degree followed the same evolutionary trend as Primates generally. There are a number of other curiously lemuroid characters in the tree-shrew which would hardly be noticed except on close examination: for example, the details of the construction of the skull, certain features of the tongue, the nose, and the small bones of the ear, and some items in the anatomy of the muscular system. If all these resemblances to the lemurs are considered, together with some evidence provided by the fossil record, there remains little doubt that the tree-shrews are properly to be regarded as exceedingly primitive members of the Order Primates.

EVOLUTION AND SPECIALIZATION IN THE PRIMATES

If, now, the various subdivisions of the Primates which we have briefly reviewed are considered as a whole, it becomes evident that they can be arranged in a sort of scale leading step by step from the very primitive tree-shrew up to Man himself. Mention has already been made of this scale in a previous section; it is an example of the *échelle des êtres* of the old French naturalists, a scale of living creatures which can be arranged in an order of increasing complexity, and which (because of the appearance of grada-tion which it demonstrates) helped to force upon biologists in the middle of last century the conception of evolution. But it must be emphasized again that this scale is not to be taken to indicate a linear sequence of evolution, for all present-day representatives of the subdivisons of the Pri-mates have undergone a greater or lesser degree of divergent specialization which to that extent has led them away from the main line of evolution culminating in the human species. The tree-shrews are much more primitively organized in their anatomical structure than lemurs, but they show certain specializations which the latter have avoided. Thus, while there are sound reasons for the statement that in their evolutionary history lemurs passed through a phase of development corresponding in the level of anatomical organization to the modern tree-shrews, the ancestors of lemurs were never precisely similar in all their structural details to the *existing* representatives of the Tupaioidea. In the same way, existing lemurs are less advanced in many of their anatomical details than tarsiers or monkeys, but they all present aberrant specializations peculiar to themselves. The tarsier, in its skull, brain and certain other features, seems to provide a link between lemurs and monkeys, but in its huge eyes and the remarkable modifications of its hind limbs it shows extreme specializations which could not possibly have been present in the ancestral stock from which the higher Primates took their origin. New World monkeys are more primitive than Old World monkeys in their den-tition, reproductive functions and other details, but they are more specialized in such features as their prehensile tails. Old World monkeys are more primitive than the existing anthropoid apes in the construction of their brains, limbs, etc., but they show certain specializations peculiar to themselves, such as the cusp pattern of their molar teeth. Finally, the existing anthropoid apes occupy a lower position in the evolutionary scale than Man by reason of the smaller size of their brain, their more primitive cranial characters, and so forth, but they also exhibit divergent specializations in certain aberrant modifications of their limbs related to rather specialized arboreal habits.

It is necessary to stress these points, since in the past a failure to recognize them has led to much fruitless controversy. For example, it has been vigorously denied that Man has ever been derived from an anthropoid ape, on the grounds that an "anthropoid ape" is an arboreal animal showing certain divergent specializations of an adaptive nature, such as are found in modern apes, and which would presumably be absent in any form ancestral to Man. But such a definition of "anthropoid ape" is far too narrow, for it only applies to certain end-products of evolution represented by the *existing* apes. The category of "anthropoid ape" must be taken to indicate not only these end-products, but also all those intermediate types which have come into existence since the progenitors of the group first became segregated in their evolutionary history from the progenitors of other groups of Primates. It is evident, from this point of view, that the earliest representatives of the anthropoid ape stock would not have manifested the structural specializations peculiar to the modern apes, and some of them, in avoiding these specializations, might well have provided a basis for the subsequent evolution of the *Hominidae*. There is certainly evidence that Man has been derived from an ancestral form whose general anatomical characters and level of organization would legitimately allow the application of the descriptive term "anthropoid ape," even though it would not have presented some of the divergent modifications shown in living apes (such as the greatly extended length of the arms, the atrophy of the thumbs, and the exaggerated development of the canine teeth).

THE EARLIEST PRIMATES

It has already been mentioned that mammals came into existence during the Mesozoic Era (perhaps as long ago as 150 million years). Indeed, there is some evidence that by the end of the Cretaceous Period they had already begun to differentiate into the several groups which are represented by the various mammalian Orders of to-day. For example, there have been found in Cretaceous deposits in Mongolia

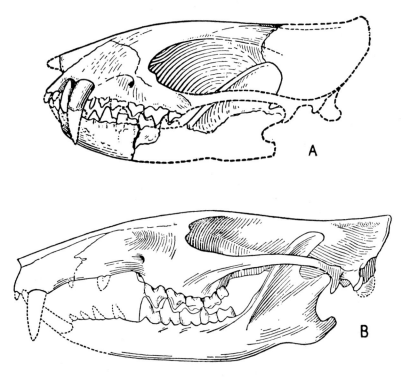

FIG. 14.—The skulls (partly reconstructed) of two Cretaceous mammals. (A) *Deltatheridium*. (B) *Zalambdalestes* (from G. G. Simpson). Twice natural size.

the skulls of exceedingly primitive mammals, of which one. *Zalambdalestes*, shows some resemblance to modern insectivores of the hedgehog group, while another, *Deltatheridium*, may represent an early precursor of the modern carnivores (Fig. 14). It is certain that, at the beginning of the Tertiary Era (about 70 million years ago), primitive mammals of great diversity of type were already very numerous, and among them were some which can be definitely recognized from their skulls and teeth as the earliest Primates.

Almost all the Primates at this remote period were quite small arboreal creatures, hardly larger than rats or mice. Many of them soon became extinct, and took no part in the evolutionary history of the modern Primates. The most primitive of all were little animals which in several details resembled the modern tree-shrews, and which are grouped in a family called the *Plesiadapidae*. So primitive and generalized in their anatomical structure are some of these little creatures, that zoologists have been in some doubt whether they could properly be regarded as Primates. But as the evidence has accumulated more and more, it has become clear that this interpretation is probably correct. It is confirmed, *inter alia*, by a comparative study of the details of the teeth, particularly the pattern of the cusps on the molar teeth. The limb bones of the plesiadapids, so far as they are known, also indicate in some of their features an affinity with the tree-shrews, and they were evidently adapted for the same kind of arboreal activity.

It will be observed that the fossil evidence fits in well with the inferences to be drawn from the indirect evidence of comparative anatomy. This is, that the earliest Primates were little tree-shrew-like creatures which at first were so primitive and generalized that they are hardly to be distinguished as Primates. It may be inferred that some of them later underwent a progressive evolutionary development (manifested particularly in the expansion of the brain, the shortening of the snout region of the skull, the modification of the limbs to serve as more efficient grasping mechanisms, and the replacement of sharp claws by flattened nails), and eventually gave rise to arboreal creatures of the lemur type. Although the fossil record of this phase of Primate evolution is still very far from complete, it does supply some direct evidence that such a transformation actually occurred, and during the latter part of the Eocene several types of lemur were already in existence in widely separate parts of the world. As we shall see, there was also an astonishing variety of tarsiers.

Fossil remains of true lemurs have been found in Eocene deposits of Europe and America. The European varieties are known by a number of well-preserved skulls, as well as by jaws and teeth and a few limb bones. Most of the fossil specimens so far known belong to a genus called *Adapis* (Fig. 15). They were about as large as modern lemurs, and showed the same specialized features in the construction of the base of the skull. On the other hand, they were much more primitive in their dental characters (they had not yet developed the dental comb which was later formed by the specialization of the lower incisors and canines), and also in the smaller size of the brain. The latter, however, had

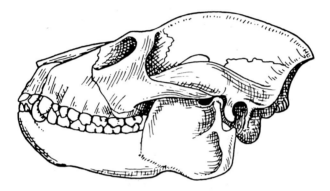

FIG. 15.—The skull of *Adapis parisiensis*, an Eocene lemur. Natural size.

already undergone a significant expansion of certain regions which were destined later to become a rather, distinctive feature of the brain of the higher Primates (forming the temporal lobes of the cerebral hemispheres). The American fossil lemurs, which are represented by skulls and teeth, and in one case by an almost complete skeleton, were very similar to their European relatives, but some of them developed certain rather peculiar specializations in the cusp pattern of their molar teeth and are included in a separate genus, *Notharctus*.

There is good reason to believe that, very soon after their appearance in the evolutionary history of the Primates, the whole group of lemurs became side-tracked on a line of their own, a line characterized by the rapid appearance of aberrant specializations of the teeth, skull and limbs which are distinguishing features of the modern lemurs. In the Eocene lemurs such specializations had not developed to more than an incipient degree, but lemuroid evolution must have proceeded rather rapidly during the ensuing Oligocene period for, by the early part of the Miocene, lemurs very similar to the modern *Galago* were already present in equatorial Africa. There is also fossil evidence that they had reached tropical Asia by Pliocene times. An important group reached Madagascar probably in the Pliocene period and, becoming isolated on that island, gave rise in Pleistocene times to a number of quite extraordinary forms which are now extinct. Among these was a giant lemur, *Megaladapis*, one of the largest Primates that ever existed (Fig. 16). There is some reason to suppose that *Megaladapis* may have survived until comparatively recent times. At any rate, a French explorer, de Flacourt, who visited Madagascar in 1658 recorded that among the animals peculiar to the island was a large creature, called by the natives the *trétrétrétré*. He described it as an animal of the size of a two-year-old calf, with a rounded head and human-like face, both fore and hind feet like those of a monkey, and ears like those of a man. It was also said to be held in great terror by the natives. It is not unlikely that the creature was actually *Megaladapis*; if so, this huge lemur was still in existence in de Flacourt's time.

The later evolution of the Pleistocene lemurs in Madagascar also gave rise to animals which were astonishingly monkey-like. Indeed, the simian appearance of the skull of one of them, *Archaeolemur*, led some zoologists to the conclusion that they actually developed into true monkeys. But a detailed study of the skull and teeth shows that the resemblance to monkeys is only superficial, for the Pleistocene lemurs of Madagascar all show certain specializations which are peculiar to the lemurs and which are absent in true monkeys. Moreover, it is now known that monkeys came into existence at a very much earlier date, at least by the Oligocene. The development of monkey-like lemurs in Madagascar is an interesting example of parallel evolution, and demonstrates a well-established principle of evolution that related groups of animals tend to develop similar characters independently. In this case (as in other cases of parallelism) a close study is sufficient to demonstrate that the resemblances are of a secondary nature, and therefore do not really indicate a very close relationship.

Besides the primitive tree-shrew-like creatures and the primitive lemurs which flourished during the Eocene period, there were a great many varieties of tarsier. We have already seen that the only modern survivor of this group is

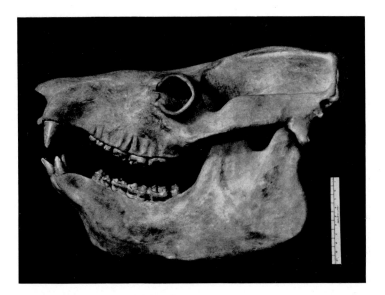

FIG. 16.—The skull of *Megaladapis*, a giant Pleistocene lemur from Madagascar. Approximately one quarter natural size.

the little tarsier which to-day inhabits Borneo, the Celebes, and the Philippine Islands. Yet in Eocene times there were at least 25 different genera spread over wide areas of the world, including Europe and America. Some of these extinct forms were very like the modern tarsier. Others (which in some of their characters are not always easily distinguishable from the Eocene lemurs) were a good deal more primitive, with smaller brains and less specialized development of the limbs and the orbital region of the skull. Still others (particularly some which inhabited the American Continent) developed aberrant specializations of the teeth of a very remarkable character. The most interesting, from the point of view of the evolution of the higher Primates, comprise a group which lived in Europe, for they showed progressive tendencies in the development of their skulls and teeth which seem to adumbrate in a significant manner the distinctive characters of monkeys. One of these was a small animal called *Necrolemur* (Fig. 13C), whose remains have been recovered from Eocene deposits in France, and another type, *Microchoerus*, used to flourish in what is now Hampshire. Some of these European tarsiers preserved a primitive type of dentition, with the full complement of teeth typical of the earliest placental mammals except for the loss of some incisors. But among them were progressive lines of evolution characterized by the early loss of the first premolar tooth, the rapid dwindling of the second, and the conversion of the last two upper premolars into bicuspid teeth closely resembling each other in shape and size. In this last character a remarkable approach was made to the sort of bicuspid premolar teeth which are typical of the higher Primates, including Man. The upper molars also became transformed from the primitive trituburcular type by the development of a fourth cusp, thus providing the quadritubercular pattern which is found in higher Primates. These evolutionary tendencies, together with other progressive changes in the construction of the bony ear-chamber of the skull, the relative shortening of the muzzle, and the expansion of the brain-case, all combine to suggest an actual transition from the tarsier phase of Primate evolution to the monkey phase. Indeed, some of the fragmentary remains which have been identified as those of Eocene tarsiers may well be found later, when more complete fossil material becomes available, to be really monkeys of a very primitive type.

The evolutionary origin of these tarsiers is still in some doubt. They may have been derived from very primitive and generalized forms of lemurs, before the ancestral lemur stock developed those specializations of structure which distinguish all the modern lemurs from the other Primates, but there are some zoologists who think it is more probable that they descended directly from tree-shrew-like ancestors without, so to speak, passing through a lemur phase. The fact is that, in the case of some of the fossil remains of the early Eocene Primates, it is a matter of great difficulty to decide whether they should be classified as lemurs or tarsiers. This sort of difficulty, of course, is to be anticipated in the study of fossil remains of transitional types in which some of the characters distinguishing two or more allied groups of existing types may be found combined in an ancestral group.

From our brief survey of the earliest Primates which were so abundant in Eocene times it is apparent that during that period there came into existence numerous kinds of small active arboreal creatures not unlike the tree-shrews of to-day, and that from these were derived several types of primitive lemurs and a diversity of tarsiers. These small Primates spread over a great part of the New World and the Old World, and many of them represent side-lines of Primate evolution which eventually became extinct. But some of the tarsiers showed a progressive trend in their development, which undoubtedly provided the basis for further evolutionary advances that later led to the appearance of true monkeys. At first sight it may seem that evolution must have proceeded with unusual rapidity during the latter part of the Eocene period, but it is to be remembered that this period lasted a long time, probably about 30 million years. From what we now know of the rate of evolutionary change, this would have provided sufficient time for the development of generalized lemurs and of progressive tarsiers from primitive tree-shrew-like ancestors.

Fossil Monkeys and Apes

The earliest and most primitive monkeys or apes of which we have any fossil remains date from the Oligocene period, perhaps about 40 million years ago. One of these is a small creature, called *Oligopithecus*, with a dentition of a generalized character but typical of the Old World Anthropoidea. Whether it is a primitive anthropoid ape, properly speaking, or an early representative of the evolutionary line leading to the cercopithecoid monkeys, is still problematical. It is known from a lower jaw which was discovered in the Fayum of Egypt, and as yet we have very little information about it. Another, still smaller, animal whose remains have been found in the same area is *Parapithecus*; it was about the size of the little squirrel monkey of to-day, and judging from its lower teeth it was very primitive indeed (Fig. 17). According to some authorities

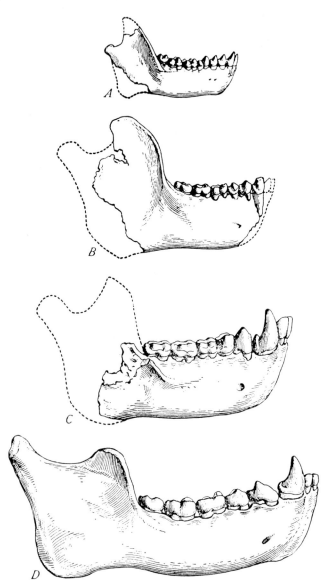

Fig. 17.—The mandibles of (A) *Parapithecus*, (B) *Proplio-pithecus*, (C) *Pliopithecus*, (D) modern gibbon. (From W. K. Gregory.) Natural size.

it had already acquired in the lower dentition the dental formula characteristic of the modern Old World monkeys and anthropoid apes—that is to say, it had two incisor teeth, a canine, two premolars and three molars. But the tooth which has been identified as the canine is relatively small and very like the premolars in shape, and the dental formula has been taken by other anatomists to be 1.1.3.3., that is to say, the same as the lower dental formula of the modern *Tarsius*. The premolar teeth are reminiscent of those of the Eocene tarsiers, while the cusp pattern of the molar teeth resembles, in a simplified form, that of anthropoid apes. The shape of the jaw as a whole is rather tarsier-like. The frontal part of a skull was later found amongst material from the same deposits and not improbably belongs to *Parapithecus*, or perhaps to *Oligopithecus*. It is quite similar in size and proportions to the skull of a marmoset. So far as it is possible to make inferences from such small fragments, *Parapithecus* and *Oligopithecus* seem to have been small monkeys or anthropoid apes of a very generalized kind, which still retained traces of their origin from a tarsioid ancestor of Eocene times. They seem also to have been sufficiently generalized to have provided a possible basis for the evolutionary development of the diverse types of anthropoid ape which appeared at a later date. Indeed, some anatomists think that *Parapithecus* may be a representative of the remote ancestral stock from which all the Hominoidea (including Man himself) were originally derived. Another rather larger creature, definitely an anthropoid ape, lived in Egypt in Oligocene times—known by a fossil jaw. This type is called *Propliopithecus* (Fig. 17). It was about the size of a small gibbon, and the teeth were in many respects similar to those of the modern gibbon. But they were simpler in construction, and the canine tooth, though it had a strong root, was not so prominent and sharp. *Propliopithecus* appears to represent a stage further than *Parapithecus* in the line of evolution leading to the anthropoid apes of to-day. These fossil specimens from Egypt, of course, provide only very scanty evidence, but they are at least sufficient to show that during the Oligocene age small monkeys and anthropoid apes of a very primitive type were already in existence. It becomes a matter of importance, therefore, that further geological deposits of this age should be carefully examined in order to secure more complete evidence of the exact nature of these ancestral forms. For there can be little doubt that in the course of evolution some of them eventually gave rise to precursors of the whole group of the Hominoidea.

One of the possible implications of the Oligocene fossils is of special interest. They suggest that the anthropoid apes may have descended directly from tarsioid ancestors without the intervention of a phase of evolution which includes the Catarrhine monkeys properly speaking. This inference has also been drawn from the results of comparative anatomical studies, for these have led to the conclusion that, in the development of certain specializations peculiar to themselves, the modern monkeys (as distinct from the anthropoid apes) represent an aberrant or side line of evolution. If this inference is correct, it is to be presumed that in their evolutionary history the Ceboidea and Cercopithecoidea diverged from the main line of evolution leading up to the anthropoid apes and Man as far back as the Early Oligocene, and perhaps earlier still.

If the fossil record indicates that small and very primitive forms of anthropoid ape were just beginning to appear in Oligocene times, it also provides evidence that in the early part of the Miocene period, probably about 25 million years ago, they had given rise to several different types which soon spread far and wide over the Old World in considerable numbers. Within recent years many remains of Early Miocene apes have been discovered in Kenya, showing quite clearly that at that time they formed a very flourishing group in the central part of Africa. They ranged from creatures of the size of a small gibbon up to large apes of gorilloid dimensions, with every intermediate grade between the two extremes. It seems that Central Africa provided in the Early Miocene a suitable environment which permitted the evolutionary development of a profusion of types, so that it became a sort of experimental breeding station for them (in the evolutionary sense). One of the smaller types of ape must have resembled the gibbon, which to-day is confined to the south-eastern part of Asia; it has been called *Limnopithecus*, but some authorities regard it as a local variant of the genus *Pliopithecus* previously known from Miocene deposits in Europe (see p. 61). Another larger type, called *Proconsul*, may possibly bear an ancestral relationship to the modern chimpanzee. The largest forms perhaps gave rise later to the gorilla.

Most of the fossil remains of extinct apes from Kenya consist of teeth and fragments of jaws. But the greater part of a skull of *Proconsul* was found in 1948, a most interesting discovery for, apart from small cranial fragments, at the time of writing it is the only known specimen of the skull of a Miocene ape (Fig. 18). In a number of features such as the smooth contour of the forehead region, the small

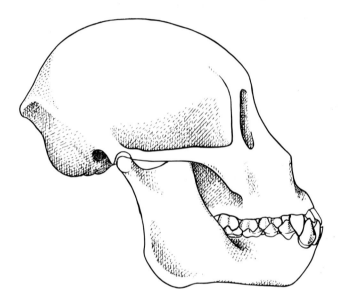

FIG. 18.—The skull of an East African Miocene ape (*Proconsul africanus*), as reconstructed by Dr. P. R. Davis and Dr. J. R. Napier.

size of the brain-case, the relatively moderate projection of the jaws, and some details of the nasal aperture, the skull is much more primitive than that of the modern African apes, and in these respects it shows certain resemblances to the Old World monkeys.

The few limb bones of these Early Miocene apes which have so far been found indicate that the larger types were of much lighter build than the modern large apes, and no doubt they were also much more agile and active. This can be inferred from the slender character of the upper limb skeleton (Fig. 19) and thigh bone, and from certain features of the ankle bones. It is also clear that they were not so specialized for brachiating habits in the trees as are the modern apes;

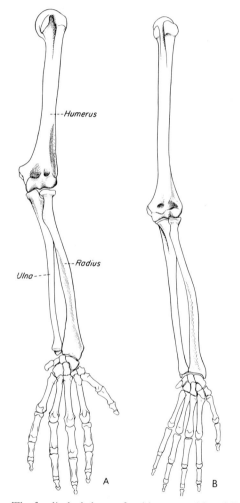

FIG. 19.—The forelimb skeleton of a chimpanzee (A) and *Proconsul africanus* (B). Both have been reduced to the same length. That of *Proconsul* is based on a reconstruction by Dr. J. R. Napier and Dr. P. R. Davis. Note the delicate construction of the limb bones in the fossil ape, the shorter forearm relatively to the upper arm, and the longer thumb.

on the contrary, they were probably much more adept at running and leaping in the manner of the quadrupedal Catarrhine monkeys. Limb bones of the smaller, gibbon-like, apes found in Kenya also show that these creatures had not developed the excessively long arms which are so characteristic of the modern gibbons. The jaws and teeth of the Early Miocene apes lacked certain of the specializations which are peculiar to the anthropoid apes of to-day and, to this extent, were actually to some degree more human in appearance. Such characters are to be expected in primitive anthropoid apes, for if modern types of anthropoid ape and Man represent lines of evolution which have diverged in the remote past from a common ancestral stock, if follows that, as their evolution is traced backwards, the lines will be found to approximate more and more, and the earliest anthropoid apes will show certain primitive features which may have been lost in the modern apes, but retained in the line of human evolution. As an example, we may mention a bony shelf which stretches across from one side of the lower jaw to the other below the region of the chin. This "simian shelf" (as it is called) is a characteristic feature of the modern large apes, though somewhat variable in the degree of its development, and is a specialization which has been developed in association with a great enlargement of the incisor teeth accompanied by a widening of the front end of the jaw. In Man there is no simian shelf; nor is it present in most Miocene apes, in which the incisor teeth still preserved their primitive dimensions.

The fossil evidence at present available suggests that the earliest evolutionary radiation of the large anthropoid apes occurred in the African continent in Early Miocene times. By the late Miocene and Early Pliocene, however, they had extended their range very considerably, for their jaws and teeth have been found in deposits of this age in several places in Europe, and also in India. A number of different genera have been recognized from these remains, the commonest being a form called *Dryopithecus*, an animal about the size of the modern chimpanzee. There was also a smaller type called *Pliopithecus* (Fig. 17) which very closely resembled the modern gibbon in the details of its dental anatomy, but which (as we now know from recent discoveries in Austria) still retained limbs of primitive proportions like those of the

Old World monkeys.   Numerous species of *Dryopithecus* have been described, and they show considerable variation in their dental anatomy, some suggesting an approach to the chimpanzee, some to the orang, and yet others to the gorilla. There can be little doubt, indeed, that among the African fossil apes and the various types of *Dryopithecus* are to be found the ancestors of all the modern large apes, or at least close relatives of these ancestors.   So far, no limb bones of *Dryopithecus* have been found, with the exception of a thigh bone (femur), and an arm bone (humerus).   Both these were discovered in Europe.   The femur has been regarded as that of an unknown giant kind of gibbon (to which the name *Paidopithex* has been given), but it almost certainly belongs to *Dryopithecus*.   It resembles quite closely the femur of the Early Miocene African apes of similar size, and shows that *Dryopithecus* was a lightly-built and agile animal.   The humerus is a slender bone, lacking the strong muscular ridges which are so often developed in the chimpanzee and gorilla for the attachment of some of the powerful arm muscles; it suggests that in *Dryopithecus* the arms had not undergone the excessive development which is to be regarded as a specialized feature of the modern anthropoid apes.

So far as the problem of the evolution of Man is concerned, it is a matter of great importance to determine whether any of the known groups of Miocene or Pliocene apes can be regarded as the actual ancestors of the human stock.   Although the fossil record is still much too incomplete to allow of a positive statement, there is reason to suppose that this may actually be so.   For example, the limb structure of some of these Miocene apes was certainly more generalized than that of the present-day apes, and may possibly have provided a basis for the development by divergent modifications of limbs of the human type as well as limbs of the type found in the modern anthropoid apes.   Again, the cusp pattern of the molar teeth of *Dryopithecus* has certain characteristic features which are not commonly found in modern Man, but which are certainly present in the teeth of fossil human types from which it is believed *Homo sapiens* may have been derived.   Some anatomists take the view, however, that the canine tooth was too large and specialized in the Miocene apes, and that the reduced form of canine tooth found in Man indicates that the hominid line of evolution must have diverged from the pongid or ape line *before* this specialization had developed. On the other hand, we have already noted that the canine tooth of modern Man shows definite traces of its derivation in the course of evolution from a tooth of larger dimensions. It is also a fact that, although no Miocene ape has yet been discovered (and many different types are now known) in which the canine was not a projecting and pointed tooth, in some species it was less prominent and less special-

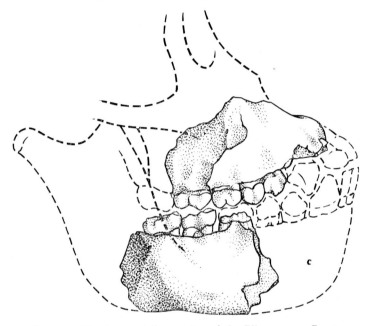

Fig. 20.—The jaws and face region of the Pliocene ape *Rama-pithecus*. Adapted from a reconstruction drawing by Professor E. L. Simons. Approximately half natural size.

ized than it is in the modern apes. Of special importance is a Pliocene hominoid, called *Ramapithecus* (Fig. 20), whose jaws and teeth have been found in India. In the small size of the teeth, the simple structure of the molars, the arcuate shape of the palate, and a number of other features, this extinct type shows a remarkable approximation to true hominids. Indeed, it has been argued with good reason that it should be included in the family *Hominidae* rather than the

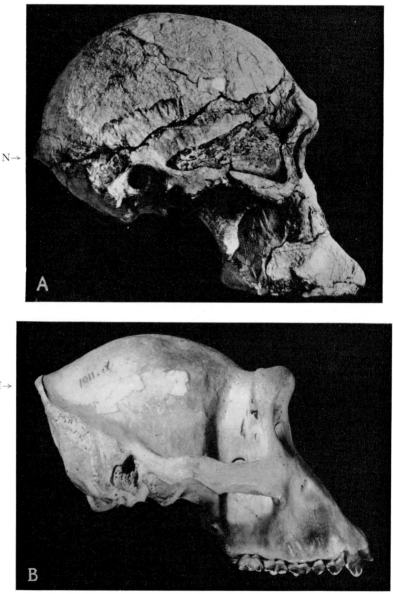

FIG. 21.—Lateral view of (A) an Australopithecine skull and (B) the skull of a female gorilla. About half nat. size. Note the contrast in the contour of the forehead, the height of the brain-case above the orbit, and the level of the nuchal crest (N).

Pongidae. If this interpretation is correct it is the earliest hominid so far known. In recent years an upper jaw with similar features of the dentition has been found in Pliocene deposits in East Africa by Dr. L. S. B. Leakey and named by him *Kenyapithecus.* But it does not appear to be distinguishable from *Ramapithecus* and should really be ascribed to this genus. It is evident, therefore, that *Ramapithecus* (like some other contemporary mammals of that time) had a wide distribution extending from South Asia to East Africa. It must be admitted, however, that the question of the anthropoid ape ancestry of Man will only be solved when we have more complete fossil remains of other parts of the skeleton besides the teeth and jaws, and the results of recent fossil-hunting expeditions permit an optimistic forecast that such evidence may be forthcoming before long.

In Lower Pliocene deposits in Italy there have been found portions of the skull and skeleton of an extinct Primate, *Oreopithecus,* which were said to show an unexpected combination of pongid and hominid features. Unfortunately, however, this important material has suffered considerable distortion in the course of fossilization which makes its anatomical study unusually difficult. It is now generally agreed, from a consideration of its limb proportions and certain unusual features of the dentition, that it more properly represents an aberrant branch of the anthropoid ape group and may conveniently be assigned to a separate family of its own, *Oreopithecidae.*

The Fossil Australopithecinae of Africa

We have seen, in the preceding section, that during Miocene and Early Pliocene times anthropoid apes of a generalized form, and showing a great diversity of type, flourished over widely distributed areas in Africa, Asia and Europe. These represented the highest level of Primate evolution which had then been attained; no Primates showing any closer approach to Man are known to have existed at so early a time. Some of these fossil apes no doubt were on evolutionary side-lines and became extinct during the Pliocene age. Others became modified and specialized to form the existing genera of anthropoid apes, of which the gibbon and orang are now confined to the south-eastern part of Asia, and the gorilla and chimpanzee to the tropical regions of Africa. Still others (for example, *Ramapithecus*) almost certainly provided the basis for the evolutionary origin of the *Hominidae*, that is to say, the zoological family which includes modern and extinct types of Man, by developing progressive tendencies such as those which were manifested in the attainment of an erect posture and in the perfection of the limbs for terrestrial progression, and by avoiding the aberrant specializations of the modern apes which are associated with their characteristic arboreal habits. We have now to consider what fossil evidence there is that such progressive forms came into existence.

In 1925 a remarkable discovery was reported by Prof. Raymond Dart, of Johannesburg. This discovery consisted of an excellently preserved portion of the skull of an immature creature of ape-like appearance, together with an almost complete natural cast of the inside of the skull, or endocranial cast. The whole of the milk dentition and also the first permanent molar teeth were in position. The specimen was embedded in a limestone matrix derived from a cave deposit at Taung near the border of Bechuanaland, South Africa. Dart called this fossil *Australopithecus*, or the Southern Ape, and he recognized in it an unexpected combination of simian features with anatomical details of a more human character.

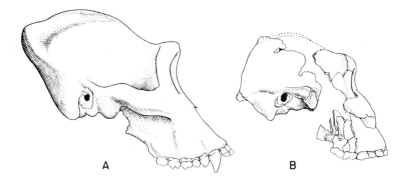

A   B

FIG. 22.—Side view of the skull of a male gorilla (A) and the Australopithecine skull ("*Zinjanthropus*") from Olduvai in Tanganyika (B), illustrating the more heavily built type of *Australopithecus*. Approximately one third natural size. (From a published photograph by Dr. L. S. B. Leakey.)

Several years later, many skulls and jaws of adult and young individuals of the same fossil group, together with some limb bones, were found by Professor Dart, the late Dr. Broom, and Dr. J. T. Robinson of the Transvaal Museum, Pretoria. They were recovered from stalagmitic limestone deposits at a number of different sites extending over considerable distances in the Transvaal. Much more recently, an unusually well preserved skull has been found in a well stratified deposit at Olduvai in Tanganyika by Dr. and Mrs. Leakey (Fig. 22). While it is recognized that all these remains belong to the same group as *Australopithecus*, it has been claimed that some of them represent different genera to which the names *Plesianthropus*, *Paranthropus*, *Telanthropus* and *Zinjanthropus* have been applied. But because it has been seriously questioned whether such generic distinctions are really justified (some authorities taking the view that the differences between them are no greater than might be expected in different species of a single genus or even different varieties of a single species) we shall here refer to them by the name of the subfamily to which they all belong, the *Australopithecinae*. The antiquity of these interesting fossils has been a matter of some doubt, for the deposits in which they were found in South Africa showed no clear stratification. But a close examination of the geological conditions under which the deposits were originally formed combined with a comparative study of the extinct types of animal whose remains have been found with them, indicates fairly certainly that the earliest specimens date from the early part of the Pleistocene period and, at the most, have an antiquity of something between half a million and one million years. By contrast, the Olduvai skull was found at a Lower Pleistocene level whose age has been estimated, by specialized methods of absolute dating, at almost two million years. It may be, therefore, that the *Australopithecinae* first appeared in East Africa, having perhaps evolved there from a Pliocene type like *Ramapithecus*, and that members of the group subsequently migrated into the Transvaal where they survived to a later date.

The general features of the *Australopithecinae* are as follows: The brain was comparable in absolute size with that of the modern large apes, and reached a volume of at least 600 cubic centimetres, and almost certainly more in the larger specimens. At the most it was only about half the average size

of the brain of *Homo sapiens*.   Probably, however, in proportion
to the size of the body as a whole, it was somewhat larger than
that of an adult male gorilla, and there is some indication (but
as yet no certainty) that the convolutional pattern on the
surface of the brain may have been a little more complicated.
The jaws were massive and projecting, and the molar teeth
were very large.   In its general proportions, indeed, the
Australopithecine skull has a superficial appearance not unlike
that of a large ape (Fig. 21), but in the details of its construction
it actually presents many differences.   For example, in some
of the better preserved skulls certain of the muscular ridges
which are so conspicuous in the skulls of the modern large apes
are much less strongly developed.   This is particularly obvious
if attention is given to the back part of the skull—the occipital
region.   In the modern apes there is a strongly developed
ridge of bone, the nuchal crest, which reaches a considerable
way up the back of the skull and serves to attach very powerful
neck muscles.   In the australopithecine skull this ridge is
situated at a much lower level, as it is in fossil human skulls of
a primitive type (Fig. 32).   The forehead region in some of
the specimens, also, is much more human in its general rounded
appearance, and while the eyebrow or supra-orbital ridges in
some skulls are heavily built, in others they are developed to
no more than a modest extent (Fig. 21).   The brain-case is set
higher in relation to the upper part of the face than it is in apes,
so that the orbital region and its relation to the zygomatic
arch have a remarkably human appearance.   This higher
"set" of the brain-case is associated with a bending upwards
of the basal axis of the skull, a feature which is well developed
in the modern human skull and in which the latter contrasts
strongly with the ape skull.   In some of the more robust and
heavily-built types of *Australopithecus* a low bony crest is
present along the mid-line of the top of the skull, the sagittal
crest, as it is called.   It serves to give additional attachment
for the large temporal muscles that are used to move the massive
lower jaw.   Superficially it may be compared with the sagittal
crest often found in some of the modern large apes, but it
differs fundamentally in that it does not extend back into
continuity with a powerfully constructed and elevated nuchal
crest (Fig. 22).

   The position of the foramen magnum and of the occipital
condyles (by which the skull articulates with the top of the

spinal column) is of particular interest.   In all the australopithecine skulls of which the basal region has been sufficiently
well preserved—and at least six of these are now available
for study—the occipital condyles are situated further forward relatively to other structures of the skull base than in
the modern large apes.   This forward position makes a significant approach to that which is characteristic of Man, and,
together with the low position of the nuchal crest, provides
some evidence that in the standing posture the skull was
habitually balanced more directly on the top of the spinal
column than it is in apes (though by no means as perfectly
as it is in *Homo sapiens.*) In other words, it suggests a bodily
posture approaching that of modern Man.   There are many
other features of the skull which are human rather than
simian, such as the conformation of the cheek bone, the shape
and design of the joint between the lower jaw and the
base of the skull, the contours of the jaws, and the way
in which certain of the skull bones articulate with each other.
Taken in combination, these comprise a "total morphological
pattern" which is not to be found in any of the known apes,
but which is, in fact, distinctive of the *Hominidae.*
   The anatomical characters of the teeth parallel those of
the skull.   The incisor teeth are relatively small, and the
canines, though in some specimens rather large and robust
in comparison with modern *Homo sapiens,* have a spatulate
shape which is typically human and very different indeed
from the sharp, projecting canines of anthropoid apes.
The front lower premolar tooth is of special significance.
In all the large apes (both fossil and Recent) it is a strong
pointed tooth in which the main part of the crown is
dominated by a single conical cusp having a cutting edge in
front.   This type of premolar (which is called a sectorial
type) is sometimes regarded as a specialization which has
secondarily developed so as to allow the tooth to work effectively against the powerful upper canine with which it comes
into contact in biting movements.   Such a modification is not
found in Man; nor was it present in the *Australopithecinae,*
in which the front lower premolar tooth has a simple bicuspid
character quite similar to that found in primitive types of
Man.
   The milk teeth of the South African fossils are also of
great interest.   The milk canines are much smaller than those

of modern apes and, in strong contrast to the latter, they have the blunt, spatulate form characteristic of Man. The first milk molar also is not a sectorial tooth of the ape type; on the contrary, it is complicated by a number of cusps set at the same general level like a human milk molar. The manner in which the permanent molar teeth became worn with use is another striking feature; the crowns became quickly ground down to an even flat surface as they quite commonly do in Man, indicating that the movements of the

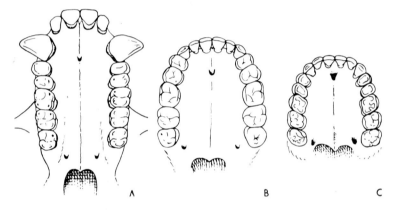

FIG. 23.—The palate and upper teeth of (A) a male gorilla, (B) *Australopithecus*, and (C) an Australian aboriginal. Note that in the curved contour of the dental arcade, the small canine teeth (worn down flat from the tip), and the absence of a gap (diastema) between the canine and incisors, the total morphological pattern consistently presented by the Australopithecine palate and upper dentition is fundamentally of the hominid type—and in sharp contrast to that of apes.

jaw in chewing were similar to those of the human jaw. Another remarkable feature is seen in the arrangement of the teeth as a whole, for they are disposed in an evenly-curved arch as in Man, and thereby show a strong contrast with the modern apes in which the grinding teeth of both sides of the jaw form parallel straight rows, ending in front in the powerful canines (see Fig. 23).

From the brief account which has just been given it is clear that the Australopithecine skull, though undoubtedly very "ape-like" in the size of the brain and in the massive projecting jaws, is in many features constructed rather on the

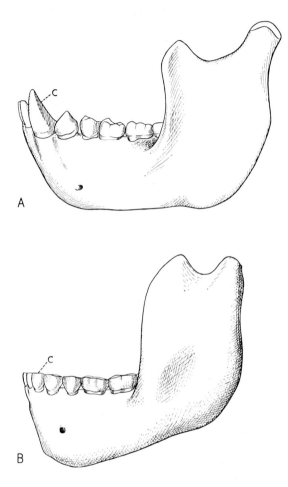

FIG. 24.—The lower jaw of (A) an anthropoid ape (orang utan) and (B) one of the *Australopithecinae*. Note that the Australopithecine canine (C) is very different from that of an ape in its shape as well as its size, and at an early stage of attrition has become worn down flat from the tip so as to be level with the other teeth (as in Man). Such a type of wear (consistently present in the *Australopithecinae*) does not occur in the anthropoid apes. Note, also, that the first premolar tooth in the Australopithecine jaw (immediately behind the canine) has not the pointed, sectorial, character which, in contrast with hominids, is quite distinctive of the ape family.

hominid plan, and that the dentition displays a complicated pattern of structural details which happens to be highly characteristic of hominids but which is not to be found in any of the known apes. There is no serious dispute about these facts, but there was at one time considerable dispute about their significance. It was argued, for example, that the *Australopithecinae* were, properly speaking, anthropoid apes of a primitive type which had *independently* developed certain anatomical characters of somewhat human appearance, but that these are, so to say, chance resemblances (the result of a process of parallel evolution), and thus are not evidence of any near relationship with Man. On the other hand, detailed studies have now made it clear that the human resemblances are too numerous, precise and detailed to be explained away in this manner, particularly in regard to such progressive features as those seen in the construction of the base of the skull and the characters of the dentition. Indeed, such a degree of evolutionary parallelism would far exceed anything that has been demonstrated to have occurred in any other mammalian sequence of evolution. But any doubts on these points were eliminated by discoveries of portions of the limb skeleton. There have so far been found in South Africa parts of the thigh bone or femur, one of the ankle bones, the upper and lower ends of the arm bone (the humerus), part of a forearm bone (the ulna) one of the small bones of the wrist, a thumb bone, a part of the shoulder blade, some of the vertebrae and ribs, and four practically complete hip bones. In one specimen the entire pelvis with the lower lumbar vertebrae and the sacrum has been preserved (Fig. 25). These limb bones are of particular importance for assessing the affinities of the South African fossils, for the reason that in their evolutionary history the limbs of the *Pongidae* (ape family) and the *Hominidae* have followed such contrasting lines of development.

The hip bones provide the most impressive evidence, partly because they are so well preserved and almost complete, and partly because no part of the skeleton is more distinctive of Man as compared with the anthropoid apes. In the apes the blade of the hip bone (the ilium) is narrow and elongated (Fig. 25). In Man it is broad and flattened in direct adaptation to the human erect posture. The broad blade provides an extensive area for the attachment of the powerful muscles of

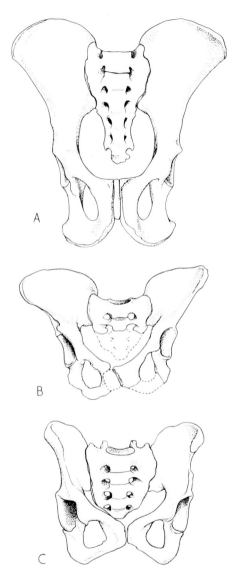

FIG. 25.—The pelvis of a chimpanzee (A), *Australopithecus* (B), and a Bushman (C). All drawn to the same scale from a photograph supplied by Professor J. T. Robinson.

the buttock, the gluteal muscles, which are used for balancing the trunk on the lower limbs in standing or walking, it gives a wider attachment to the abdominal muscles which are so important for maintaining abdominal tone in the standing position, and it also plays a part in supporting the abdominal viscera in the upright posture. In the shape of the ilium, the *Australopithecinae* appear to be almost entirely human and show no close resemblance to the ape. From this anatomical evidence it has been inferred that, although they probably were not capable of the striding gait that is so typical of *Homo sapiens*, these fossil creatures stood and walked almost as Man does to-day, and this inference (it will be noted) is in entire conformity with the conclusions drawn from the position of the occipital condyles on the base of the skull. It also harmonizes with the evidence of the femur. The details of the joint surfaces of the lower end of the femur, taken in combination with each other and with the slope of the lower part of the shaft of the bone, also show hominid characters which are related to the erect posture.

The ankle bone found at one of the South African australo-pithecine sites provides an interesting combination of human and simian features. It is the bone (called the talus) through which the weight of the body is transferred from the tibia to the rest of the foot. The upper joint surface (which articulates with the lower end of the tibia) shows hominid characters in its relative breadth and its even curvature from side to side. The joint surface at the front end (head) of the bone is remarkable for its wide extent from side to side, reaching inwards to a degree which resembles the ape rather than Man. It may be suggested that, whereas the main part of the bone is constructed for stability in weight-bearing in a standing position, the broad curvature of the head is related to a greater mobility of the fore part of the foot than is possible in modern Man.

As regards the upper limb, the humerus and ulna fragments are of delicate build, and lack the powerful muscular ridges so often found in the brachiating apes. They appear to be quite closely similar to those of Man, and it is probable that, if they had been found alone, they would have been regarded as human bones.

It is now necessary to make mention of further discoveries by Dr. L. S. B. Leakey at Olduvai in Tanganyika; these consist of hominid bones and teeth found in the same general area as the australopithecine skull to which the name "*Zinjanthropus*" had been given, and at approximately the same geological level. The remains include parietal bones and a frontal bone of the skull, jaws and teeth, two bones of the shin (tibia and fibula), an almost complete foot skeleton, and some finger and wrist bones. It has been suggested that most, if not all, of these remains are not those of an australopithecine but belong to a more advanced type that should be included (like modern man) in the genus *Homo*.

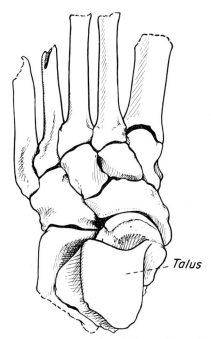

Talus

FIG. 26.—Upper aspect of the foot skeleton of one of the australopithecines found at Olduvai in Tanganyika. The front ends of the metatarsal bones and the back end of the heel bone (calcaneus) are missing. Approximately three-quarters natural size. (From a photograph supplied by Dr. M. A. Day and Dr. J. R. Napier.)

Accordingly, the type was christened "*Homo habilis*". But this interpretation has been strongly contested by some authorities on the ground that all the specimens conform much more closely in their anatomical characters with the genus

Australopithecus than with any known type, modern or extinct, of *Homo*. For example, the intracranial capacity has been computed on the rather insecure evidence of fragmentary and fragmented parietal bones to have been about 680 c.c., that is, within estimations for the australopithecine range and well below that of *Homo*. The foot skeleton, though very like that of modern man, is said to indicate that the transmission of weight to the foot was somewhat different and that the striding gait of *Homo sapiens* had not yet been achieved—inferences also consistent with those drawn from the pelvis of the South African australopithecines. Indeed, the talus (Fig. 26), shows some unusual features in which it resembles the talus previously found with australopithecine remains in South Africa. The teeth, though relatively small, are not outside the range of variation of size in *Australopithecus*. The finger bones, in their robust and strongly curved character agree very well with the strongly curved thumb bone (metacarpal) found at one of the australopithecine sites of the Transvaal. Further, the Olduvai wrist bone that articulates with the thumb shows certain gorilloid features that parallel similar gorilloid features of the australopithecine metacarpal from South Africa (though both make it clear that the thumb was opposable for grasping purposes in a manner characteristic of the human thumb). And lastly, the tibia and fibula, in spite of their obvious hominid traits, do show primitive features that are not characteristic of *Homo*. In general, then, it may be said that the skeletal features of these ancient fossil remains are not only not incompatible—they are positively compatible—with *Australopithecus*. We shall therefore take the view here that "*Homo habilis*" is more properly to be regarded as a variant, or perhaps a local species, of the genus *Australopithecus*, only differing from the South African representatives of this group in rather minor details that indicate a more generalized stage of development. Nevertheless, it needs to be recognized that this question of the nomenclature of the Olduvai fossils is still a matter of controversy, and perhaps is likely to remain so until more complete skeletal material comes to light.

So human in their general appearance and combination of anatomical details are the limb bones of the *Australopithecinae* that at first the question naturally arose whether perhaps they might not be parts of a relatively modern human skeleton, which had somehow become mixed up with the skulls and teeth of extinct ape-like creatures. In other words, did the limb bones, skulls and teeth really all belong to the same creatures? The discoveries in South Africa gave quite a clear answer to this question. For example, some of the hip bones, and also other limb-bones, ribs and vertebrae, have been found in the same limestone matrix in direct association with skulls and teeth of the *Australopithecinae*. No skulls or teeth of *Homo sapiens* have been found in these deposits (in spite of the careful examination of hundreds of tons of the limestone matrix), and no other kinds of limb bones have been found which can be related to the skulls and teeth of the *Australopithecinae*. It is now certain, therefore, that these fossil creatures were equipped with limbs rather similar to those of Man, and quite distinct from those characteristic of modern apes. Thus there can be no doubt that the *Australopithecinae*, in spite of their small brains and large jaws, were capable of standing and walking approximately in human fashion. It is interesting to note that this conclusion is entirely consistent with the climatic evidence. For this indicates that the *Australopithecinae* lived, not in a forest environment like modern anthropoid apes, but in a relatively more arid environment, and they must presumably, therefore, have been well adapted for terrestrial life.

Finally, it should be mentioned that the limb-bone remains of the *Australopithecinae* so far discovered are mostly of small dimensions, indicating that in stature some of these creatures were about the size of the pygmy races of Man to-day.

The large quantity of skulls, bones and teeth which have been collected in Africa now allows us to construct a fairly complete picture of the *Australopithecinae*. They were hominids of generally small stature, with a brain not much larger in absolute size than that of most large gorillas, a massive jaw showing a number of human characters, a skull in which many of the structural details conform to the hominid rather than the ape pattern, a dentition fundamentally of human type (in spite of the large size of the premolar teeth and the permanent molars) and lacking the tusk-like canines and large incisors of the modern anthropoid apes, an opposable thumb, and limbs approximating in their structure and proportions to those of *Homo*. Undoubtedly the most surprising feature of their whole anatomy is the combination of a brain of simian dimensions with limbs which, in a number

of details, are of human type, and it was this apparent contra-
diction which led some anatomists in the first instance to
doubt the validity of the evidence provided by the South
African fossils. The more recent discoveries, however, have
added so much more evidence of a confirmatory nature that
any such doubts have now been removed.

It is now clear that at least by the early part of the Pleistocene age (and perhaps even earlier) the line of hominid
evolution had led to the development of limbs approximating
to the human type, even though the brain was still comparatively small. In other words, the evolutionary development
of the limbs appears to have outstripped that of the brain.
But this phenomenon seems to have been a common feature
of Primate evolution. In some of the Eocene lemurs, for
example, the limbs had already become closely approximated
in their structure to those of modern lemurs while the brain
was still far more primitive, and, as we shall see, in certain
fossil remains of extinct types of Man, which show a
brain of a distinctly primitive type, the limb bones (so far
as they are known) were apparently indistinguishable from
those of *Homo sapiens* of to-day. It appears, indeed, that in
the process of human evolution the expansion and elaboration of the brain followed, and were perhaps conditioned by,
the perfection of the limbs for an erect mode of progression.

The question now arises, what is the proper place of the
Australopithecinae in the classification of the higher Primates?
It is widely agreed that they should be grouped with the
Hominidae rather than with the anthropoid ape family
(*Pongidae*) for, as we have seen, they show a great number of
anatomical characters which (taken in combination) indicate that they have developed in a direction corresponding
to the hominid line of evolution, and quite opposite to the
direction followed by the pongid line of evolution. It has
indeed been argued that the small size of the brain in the
Australopithecinae brings them into the zoological category
of "apes" but, in fact, this is not a valid criterion for it is
certain that in the earlier representatives of the *Hominidae*
(and for some time after this family had become segregated
from the *Pongidae* in their evolutionary divergence from
a common ancestral stock) the brain had not become
expanded to the dimensions of modern Man. But, apart
from the question of brain size, the evidence of skull struc-

ture, dental anatomy and the details of the pelvis and limb bones, establishes fairly clearly that the *Australopithecinae* are to be regarded as exceedingly primitive representatives of the family which includes modern and extinct types of Man. The question whether the terms "Man" and "human" can be appropriately applied to the South African fossils must depend on evidence that these creatures possessed attributes commonly associated with the status of humanity such as the ability to speak and to fabricate tools. Quite recently a number of crude stone artifacts have been found in association with remains of the *Australopithecinae* at more than one site in South Africa, and of particular importance in this connection is the site at Olduvai where australopithecine remains were found embedded in a living floor side by side with stone implements of the pebble-tool type and some of the flakes struck off in their fabrication. We have already noted that the australopithecine hand possessed an opposable thumb, and it has been inferred from this that, anatomically speaking, the hand was certainly capable of fabricating stone or bone implements of a simple kind. It may be noted also that, at the original site at Taung, where the first australopithe-cine skull was discovered, a number of baboon skulls were found showing depressed fractures on the top, which suggests that they were killed by well-aimed blows with a weapon of some sort, and it has been surmised from this evidence that baboons were systematically hunted for food by the *Austra-lopithecinae*.

Finally the question arises whether the zoological group to which the South African fossils belong is likely to bear any direct or indirect ancestral relationship to *Homo sapiens*. A careful analysis of all the purely anatomical data brings to light no serious grounds for precluding such a possi-bility. Indeed, it is possible to go further and to affirm that the anatomical characters of the *Australopithecinae* conform very closely to theoretical postulates for an intermediate stage of human evolution, which had been primarily based on the indirect evidence of comparative anatomy. But the place occupied by these fossils in the evolutionary history of Man will be precisely determined only when more evidence becomes available to trace their relationship to other early hominids whose fossil remains have been reported from Africa. There is good reason to suppose that already by

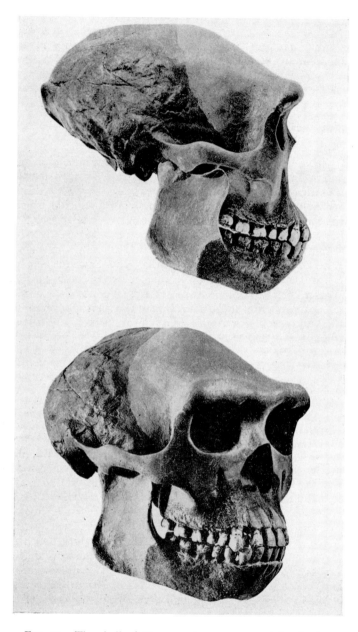

Fig. 27.—The skull of *Homo erectus* reconstructed by the late
Dr. F. Weidenreich from remains in Java. Approximately
one-third natural size.

the early Pleistocene they had undergone some degree of structural diversification to form different geographical varieties or even different species, and this may be taken to imply that, as a group, the *Australopithecinae* must have been in existence still earlier, i.e., at the end of the Pliocene. This inference needs to be susbstantiated by more direct geological evidence; if it proves correct, it would clearly place the group in a chronological position appropriate for an ancestral group.

HOMO ERECTUS

In the preceding sections we have traced the gradual evolutionary advance of the higher Primates, the Hominoidea, by reference to the fossil remains of anthropoid apes of generalized types in the Miocene and Pliocene periods, and to the remarkable African *Australopithecinae*. As we have seen, the latter, in spite of their ape-like appearance, showed many characters which had previously been regarded as quite distinctive of Man. It is now necessary to make clear in our minds what exactly is meant by the terms "Man" and "human" in reference to hominid evolution. Here we shall limit them to those representatives of the family *Hominidae* which had acquired a level of intelligence enabling them to fabricate tools and implements—in other words, we shall adopt the definition of Man as a tool-making creature. Thus, since there is as yet no certain evidence that there were any precursors of the *Australopithecinae* who made tools, such hypothetical precursors may conveniently be referred to the "pre-human phase of hominid evolution". Apart from the *Australopithecinae* some of the earliest fossil records of true Man, that is, of hominoids which not only come within the family of the *Hominidae* but were intelligent enough to fabricate stone implements, have been found in the Far East. The story of their discovery is as follows:

Over seventy years ago a Dutch anthropologist named Dubois discovered in Central Java portions of a skeleton which aroused acute discussion among students of human evolution. They included a skull cap and a thigh bone. The skull cap might have belonged to a very primitive type of man, but it showed remarkable ape-like characters in its general flattened shape, its enormous eye-brow prominences, the complete absence of what is usually called a forehead, and the small size of the brain-case (Figs. 27 and 28). On the other hand, the thigh bone, in its shape and proportions, was obviously adapted mechanically for the same kinds of stress and strain for which a modern human thigh bone is adapted; its owner evidently stood erect and walked much as we do to-day. The creature to whom these skeletal fragments belonged was called by its discoverer *Pithecanthropus erectus*, or the "ape-man with an erect posture". Some anatomists believed it to be really a giant gibbon, others that it was a real man, but of exceedingly primitive type, and yet others saw in it the "missing link"—half-way between ape and man. The last interpretation seemed to accord with the size of the brain-case (which gives a close indication of the size of the actual brain). The capacity of the brain-case of this first specimen of

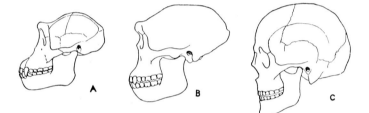

FIG. 28.—Side view of the skull of (A) a chimpanzee, (B) *Homo erectus* (as reconstructed by the late Dr. Weidenreich), and (C) *Homo sapiens*.

Pithecanthropus was estimated to be about 900 cubic centimetres, which is approximately intermediate between the average skull capacity of the largest living apes (about 500 c.c.) and that of modern Man (about 1350 c.c.). Thus it appears that the brain of *Pithecanthropus* was intermediate between modern apes and modern Man in point of size, even though it must be admitted that exceptionally small brains, corresponding to a cranial capacity of 1000 c.c. or even less, do occasionally occur as extreme normal variations in modern Man. In the years preceding the last war new discoveries of the highest importance were made in the Far East which have given us much more certain knowledge of *Pithecanthropus*. They have also led to the realization that, after all, these early hominids were not so different from later and modern types of man as to warrant a generic distinction. On the other hand it is agreed that they do constitute a distinct species of the genus *Homo*, and thus the term *Pithecanthropus erectus* has now been replaced by *Homo erectus*.

In 1936 and during the three following years further remains of *Homo erectus* came to light in Java. The new discoveries comprised a large portion of a massive lower jaw with several of the teeth in position, an adult skull (much more complete than the original skull-cap), the back portion of another skull with a considerable part of the upper jaw and teeth, part of the roof of a third skull, and the skull of an infant. This last discovery, of a baby *Homo erectus*, is of the greatest interest. It was found at a place called Modjokerto in Central Java (not far from the site of the original discovery in 1891), and from its ana-

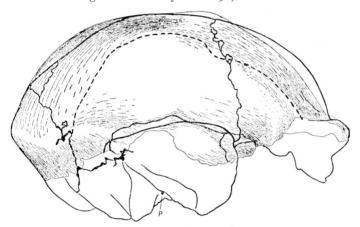

FIG. 29.—A skull cap of *Homo erectus* found in Java on which is superimposed the outline of one of the skulls found in China. Half natural size. The two are closely similar, but in the Chinese variant of *Homo erectus* the forehead region is better developed. *p* marks the position of the bony aperture of the ear. (From F. Weidenreich.)

tomical characters probably belonged to an infant of two years of age, or perhaps a little older. Compared with the skulls of modern children of an equivalent age it is small (Fig. 31), for its cranial capacity is estimated at about 700 c.c. (in comparison with about 1000 c.c. for a modern European child of two years), and by reference to data concerning the brain growth of modern Man and the anthropoid apes it may be inferred that the capacity would probably

not have expanded beyond 1000 c.c. in the adult.   The brow
ridges already at this early age are unusually prominent, and
the forehead region (which in apes as well as Man is relatively
more prominent in the infant than it is in the adult) is
definitely retreating.

Finally, mention should be made of a small portion of a
lower jaw with three teeth, which was found in Central Java
in 1941.   The general features of this fossil fragment con-

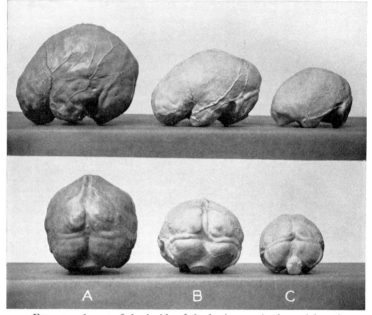

FIG. 30.—A cast of the inside of the brain-case (endocranial cast)
of (A) *Homo sapiens*, (B) *Homo erectus* and (C) chimpanzee.
Side view above, back view below.   A little more than one-sixth
natural size.

form with those of *Homo erectus*, but it is of enormous size.
It has therefore been claimed to represent a different genus of
extinct Man, called *Meganthropus*; it has even been interpreted,
on the basis of its tooth structure, as an Asian representative
of the *Australopitheciae*.   However, it seems more reasonable
to suppose that the jaw really belonged to an unusually large
individual of the *Homo erectus* group.   In this connexion, it is
well to recognize that the range of variation in size and shape
of the teeth in both *Australopithecus* and *Homo erectus* was

quite considerable, with overlapping between the two genera, and in some cases it may not be possible to distinguish with certainty one from the other on dental morphology alone. For example, the generic term *Telanthropus* was originally applied to some very incomplete jaw fragments and teeth found in australo-pithecine deposits in the Transvaal, and their relatively small size later led to the suggestion that they indicated the presence of *Homo erectus* living contemporaneously with *Australopithecus*. But, again, there seems to be no good evidence that the size of the teeth and jaws were outside the range of variation in the australopithecines. Both in the case of "*Meganthropus*" and "*Telanthropus*" much more complete skeletal material (par-ticularly the skull and limb bones) is required to establish their true significance.

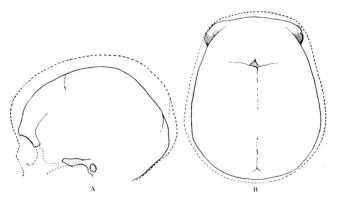

A   B

Fig. 31.—The outline of the brain-case of a baby *Homo erectus* (found at Modkokerto in Java) superimposed on that of a modern European child (interrupted line) of two years. In (A) skulls are viewed from the side and in (B) from above. Approximately one-third natural size.

Let us now turn our attention to the Chinese village of Choukoutien, situated about 40 miles south-west of Pekin. In 1927 excavations carried out in caves at Choukoutien (under the direction of a Canadian anatomist, the late Prof. Davidson Black) brought to light a single molar tooth of primitive human type. The anatomical features of this tooth were deemed to be sufficiently distinctive to justify the inference that it must have belonged to an extinct type of Man, and to this type the name "*Sinanthropus*" (Man of China) was given. This conclusion met with a good deal of scepticism among anatomists generally, mainly because the sort of evidence provided by a single tooth seemed to be rather insecure. However, two years later other discoveries were made which vindicated the original contention that the tooth was of quite an unusual character. Continued excavations led to the discovery, in 1929, of a fairly complete skull, together with portions of jaws and teeth. During the next few years (until the Japanese invasion of China stopped all further work) the remains of more skulls were found, as well as large numbers of teeth and some fragments of limb bones. Indeed, there eventually became available for study skulls, or portions of skulls, from Choukoutien of at least fourteen individuals, young and old, with teeth and fragments of jaws belonging to more than forty individuals, as well as the shafts of two thigh bones and an upper arm bone, a collar-bone and one of the wrist bones.

Both the Javanese and the Chinese fossils have a considerable antiquity. The former are estimated to date back to the earlier part of the Middle Pleistocene, probably almost half a million years ago. The latter probably date from the latter part of the Middle Pleistocene.

It has already been mentioned that when the Chinese fossils were first discovered they were allocated to a special type of extinct man, *Sinanthropus*. However, comparative studies have now made it quite clear that they really represent the same general type as the Javanese fossils (Fig. 29), and it is therefore evident that they should both be included in the common species, *Homo erectus*. At the same time they show certain differences of a relatively minor character which may be sufficient to indicate that they belonged to different subspecies. The original name given to the fossil man found by Dubois, *Pithecanthropus erectus*, was intended to indicate that, as the evidence of the thigh bone seemed to show, this primitive hominid walked in an erect attitude like modern Man. The Chinese fossil remains have served to confirm this inference.

After the death of Prof. Davidson Black the systematic study of the Choukoutein fossils was carried on by the late Dr. Weidenreich, who has described them in great detail in a series of outstanding monographs. The more recently discovered remains of *Homo erectus* in Java have been studied by

Dr. von Koenigswald. The information which they provide has tended to emphasize the human rather than the simian character of *Homo erectus*. At the same time, as we shall see, this extinct type of Man did show some very remarkable ape-like features.

One unexpected result of the study of the *Homo erectus* material is the variability observed in the brain-size. In five of the Chinese skulls it was found to vary from 850 c.c. to 1300 c.c. (with an average of 1075 c.c.), while in three of the Javanese skulls it ranges from 775 c.c. to 900 c.c. (with an average of 860 c.c.). Thus the Javanese "ape-man" seems to have possessed a distinctly smaller brain, and in this respect was clearly the more primitive of the two. The average of all the *Homo erectus* material comes to approximately 1000 c.c., as compared with 1350 c.c. for modern human races. No doubt the small brain size is partly correlated with the fact that individuals of this ancient species were rather undersized individuals by modern standards (their average height was probably not much more than five feet), but it cannot be altogether explained on this basis. For example, the average cranial capacity of the modern Bushman, whose average height is rather less than five feet, is about 1300 c.c. A number of anatomists have attempted to learn more about the brain of *Homo erectus* by studying endocranial casts made from the inside of the skull. These give information on the shape and relative dimensions of the different parts of the brain, and also give faint indications of the pattern of some of the foldings, or convolutions, of the grey matter on the surface. Unfortunately, however, there is practically nothing which we can learn about the quality or the specific functions of the brain by this method. As regards general proportions, however, a glance at Fig. 30, which shows endocranial casts of *Homo erectus* compared with those of a chimpanzee and a modern man, will make it clear that the fossil "ape man" does occupy a position which is in many respects intermediate between the two others.

In association with the small size of the brain, the skull of *Homo erectus* shows many lowly characters (Figs. 27 and 28). The heavy and prominent eyebrow ridges first attract attention, and are strongly reminiscent of those found in the gorilla and chimpanzee. They are continued across the mid-line above the root of the nose to form a continuous projecting shelf, and in this respect (apart from their size) are quite different from the eyebrow ridges seen in modern Man. The forehead region slopes gradually upwards and

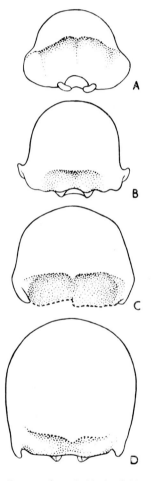

F<small>IG</small>. 32.—The skulls, seen from behind, of (A) a chimpanzee, (B) one of the *Australopithecinae*, (C) *Home erectus* and (D) *Homo sapiens*. The skulls have all been orientated with reference to the same standard plane. (By permission of the Chicago University Press.) Note the high level of the nuchal crest in the chimpanzee skull—a characteristic feature of the anthropoid ape family (*Pongidae*).

backwards from the eyebrow ridges, and only in the Pekin skulls is there developed in some cases a rounded prominence which can be properly termed a "forehead". The back of the skull is rather sharply pointed (instead of being evenly rounded, as it is in *Homo sapiens*), and it has an extensive area for the attachment of what must have been very powerful neck muscles. As seen from behind, the whole brain-case is flattened from above downwards, with its width greater than its height and its widest part at the base (as in the anthropoid apes). In modern Man, on the other hand, the widest part of the brain-case is usually in the parietal region of the skull, that is, considerably above the level of the base, and, viewed from behind, its height is commonly greater than its width (Fig. 32).

The nose of *Homo erectus* was broad and flat, as it is in certain races of mankind to-day. The jaws were massive and markedly prognathous, that is to say, they projected forwards in muzzle-fashion considerably beyond the level of the nose and the rest of the face. As in apes, also, there is no chin in the ordinary sense, for the front of the lower jaw retreats backwards from the level of the incisor teeth. In a number of points the teeth show simian features—their size, the massiveness of the canine tooth and its rather late appearance during the "cutting" of the teeth in the growing child, and some details of the pattern of the crowns of the molars. Yet, in spite of these primitive characters of the jaws and teeth, they are seen to be essentially human in their general conformation when compared with these structures in modern apes. For example, the teeth are arranged in an even curve (as in the *Australopithecinae*), whereas in modern apes, as we have already noted, the grinding teeth of either side are disposed in parallel, straight rows ending in front in the sharp projecting canines (see Fig. 23A). Again, though the canines in *Homo erectus* in some cases are rather pointed and project beyond the level of the crowns of the other teeth (particularly in the Javanese representatives of this extinct race) they are approached in these characters by the canines of some modern individuals.

We have mentioned above that some limb bones of *Homo erectus* have been found, though unfortunately they are few and fragmentary. Yet they are sufficient to demonstrate that, in spite of the primitive character of the skull, brain and teeth, the limbs seem to have been similar in their shape, proportions and fine modelling to those of present-day Man. Thus, as the evidence of the australopithecine fossils also suggests, the limbs of prehistoric man must have reached the completion of their evolutionary development long before the skull, brain and teeth. The limb bones of *Homo erectus*, besides giving evidence of a gait and posture as advanced as that of modern Man, indicate a total standing height of not much more than about five feet.

We are now in a position to form a mental picture of the general appearance of *Homo erectus* when he was alive. He was rather short in stature by modern standards, with limbs fashioned as they are to-day, but with heavy beetling brows, a very retreating forehead, powerful jaws equipped with rather large teeth, and powerfully developed neck muscles. It may also be presumed, on account of the small average size of the brain, that he had a relatively low level of intelligence. However, implements of quartz and other material found with his skeletal remains in the caves at Choukoutien show that he was intelligent enough and skilful enough to fabricate these tools, in spite of the fact that quartz is by no means an easy material to manipulate for this purpose. There has also been found in the same caves evidence of numerous hearths, indicating that he knew how to use fire, as well as charred bones of animals bearing witness to his culinary activities. Further, he was evidently a great hunter, for 70 per cent. of the animal remains found at one site belong to deer. Lastly, it has been suggested that he practised cannibalism, since several of the skulls of the Chinese fossils show signs of injury, as though their owners had met with a violent death, and they are broken in a fashion which leads to the supposition that this was done in order to extract the brain. Possibly, however, this ancient "ape-man" indulged in customs somewhat similar to those of the head hunters of modern times in Borneo and elsewhere.

All these activities seem to make it clear that, culturally, *Homo erectus* may have been almost as advanced as some of the less civilized races of mankind to-day. It is, in any case, a striking fact that, so long ago as the Middle Pleistocene, primitive types of Man were in existence who had already discovered the domestic use of fire, and were capable of manufacturing their stone tools.

The evolutionary relationship of *Homo erectus* to modern Man, *Homo sapiens*, seems fairly clear, for there are now available many remains of prehistoric Man which seem, from the anatomical point of view, to provide a graded series linking the two. In the following sections we shall deal with some of the evidence for this general statement.

THE PLEISTOCENE PERIOD AND THE ORIGIN OF *HOMO SAPIENS*

The highly technical procedures used for the absolute dating of geological deposits and their contained fossils have lately made it clear that the beginning of the Pleistocene period was much earlier than had previously been supposed; probably it began almost three million years ago. But the date of the transition from the Pliocene to the Pleistocene Period is really an arbitrary point of time, and geologists have not found it easy to agree on the definition of this arbitrary point. Broadly speaking, it was marked by the gradual onset of a cooler climate in many parts of the world, accompanied by the appearance of certain mammals approximating more closely than their Pliocene predecessors to those of today, and the general lowering of the temperature finally led to the Great Ice Age, during which ice-caps, originating on highlands, spread out over lowlands in the temperate zones. This process of glaciation was a recurrent phenomenon which extended throughout the latter part of the Pleistocene Period. It is now generally agreed that there were four main glacial periods, of varying duration and different degrees of severity, separated by interglacial periods during which the climate became much warmer. Traces of the successive glaciations can be detected by the study of the characteristic geological deposits left by melting ice and so forth, and also by reference to the fossil remains of the animals and plants which inhabited the neighbourhood of the glaciated regions. These animals and plants belonged to types which were particularly adapted for life in a cold environment. The mammals, for example, included the mammoth, woolly rhinoceros, musk-ox, reindeer and arctic fox among others. On the other hand, the geological deposits laid down in the warm interglacial periods contain the fossil remains of animals and plants adapted for a warmer climate, including mammals such as the hippopotamus and the straight-tusked elephant

(*Elephas antiquus*). As the ice-sheets spread southwards over North-West Europe with the onset of each glaciation, the warm climate fauna and flora migrated elsewhere and were replaced by cold climate types. With the retreat of the glaciers the opposite process took place.

By their determination of the rhythmical succession of glacial and interglacial phases during the Pleistocene Period, geologists have provided a sort of time scale by reference to which it is possible to infer the *relative* antiquity of the fossil remains of prehistoric Man, or of the stone implements which he left behind. For if the deposits laid down during the various glacial and interglacial periods can be placed in a regular temporal sequence on purely geological evidence, any fossils found in these deposits can likewise be placed in their proper sequence. Attempts have been made, using various sources of evidence, to calculate the actual antiquity in years of the various glaciations. For example, according to provisional estimates, the first glaciation began about 600,000 years ago, the second about 500,000 years, the third about 250,000 years and the fourth about 70,000 years. The last glaciation reached its final climax and began to terminate about 20,000 years ago. It should be emphasized, however, that there is as yet no certainty regarding the precision of this absolute chronological scale, and it should be regarded as only a rough approximation.

Finally, it should be noted that even in those parts of the world (e.g. Central Africa) where there was no actual glaciation, climatic fluctuations of a different type occurred, and there appear to have been a succession of alternating rainy and dry periods. It may be possible to equate these pluvial and interpluvial phases with the glacial and interglacial periods in the northern hemisphere whose approximate antiquity has been established. The importance of determining such a correlation is clear, for it would permit definite conclusions regarding the time relationships of human fossils found in widely different parts of the world.

Fossil remains of early Man are unfortunately but rarely found. On the other hand, the stone implements which he manufactured are often discovered in large numbers. We are not concerned here with the details of the various types of artifacts which he developed during the final stages of his evolutionary progress, but it is necessary to make a very brief reference to them because of the collateral evidence they provide in the study of the origin of *Homo sapiens.*

No indisputable evidence of manufactured implements is available from any deposits of Pliocene date. So far as is known for certain, they first appear in the early part of the Pleistocene. Some of the very early implements were large nodules or flakes of stone which had been crudely shaped by coarse chipping to form rough hand axes or choppers. Later, as more refined techniques were developed, the implements took on a more regular form and showed a more perfect finish. They were also produced in greater variety, different tools being designed for different purposes, and easily recognizable as knives, scrapers, borers and so forth. Throughout the Pleistocene, stone tools were fashioned entirely by chipping; the art of shaping stone implements by grinding and polishing was not discovered till later, in what is called the Neolithic Age, which began less than 7000 years ago. The prolonged period during which the chipping technique was slowly developed and perfected is called by archaeologists the Palaeolithic or Old Stone Age, and the early types of Man who were responsible for its development are sometimes referred to as Palaeolithic Man.

Different groups of Palaeolithic Man, at different times and in different places, tended to develop their own distinctive methods of chipping and flaking, and to fabricate implements of characteristic types. Thus it has been possible to recognize and distinguish a number of different stone "industries," each of which is now known to have been characteristic of a particular phase of cultural evolution and, in some cases, to have been associated with a particular physical type of Palaeolithic Man. Further, it is possible to place these industries in a temporal sequence (even though one type of industry may have overlapped another in a different geographical area), and to relate this sequence to the succession of glacial and interglacial phases in the Pleistocene period. For a general account of the successive Palaeolithic cultures in Europe and other parts of the world, with a table illustrating their chronological sequence, reference should be made to "Man the Toolmaker" by K. P. Oakley.

The main palaeolithic industries, whose succession during the Pleistocene Period has been studied particularly in

Europe, are as follows. They are named after the places where they were first discovered and defined in detail. The correlation in time of these various industries with the several cold and warm cycles of the Pleistocene is based on geological evidence, and in some degree is to be regarded as a provisional correlation until this evidence is more complete.

As we have already seen (p. 79), there is good evidence that the *Australopithecinae* were capable of making crude pebble tools, and the latter, because they were first described from deposits at Olduvai, comprise what is termed the Oldowan industry. A later, but still primitive, industry, the Abbevillian (sometimes called Chellean), persisted over a great interval of time corresponding to the second glacial period and onset of the following interglacial period. It was mainly characterized by large hand-axes of crude form. It was succeeded by the Acheulian industry, which lasted until the third interglacial period. In this industry the hand-axes reached a more perfect form and were provided with a more effective cutting edge. The Levalloisian and Mousterian industries date back to the third interglacial period and the early stages of the fourth or last glacial period. The flaking and chipping of the implements characteristic of these industries were more elaborate and carefully done than in the preceding periods, and it was common for tools to be made from large flakes which had previously been struck off specially prepared "cores" of flint. As far as is known, also, it was in Mousterian times that ceremonial burial was first practised. During the final stages of the last glacial period highly developed cultures termed the Aurignacian, Solutrean and Magdalenian followed each other. The people of the Aurignacian period manufactured many types of implements of excellent design and showing fine workmanship. They also made use of material such as bone, horn and ivory, and designed necklaces and other personal ornaments. But perhaps their greatest distinction was the development of a remarkable artistic aptitude which was expressed in beautiful cave drawings and sculptures. In the Solutrean period, "pressure flaking"—a technique whereby small flakes can be removed with great precision and accuracy— was developed to a high pitch of excellence, and made it possible to produce fine javelin blades of great delicacy and beauty. Finally, in the Magdalenian period, the stone tools were supplemented by a great variety of characteristic implements carved from reindeer antler, such as harpoons, lance heads, and spear throwers. The Magdalenian culture

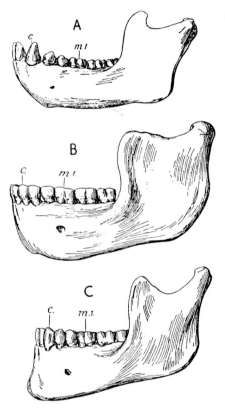

Fig. 33.—The Heidelberg mandible (B), compared with the mandible of a chimpanzee (A) and modern Man (C). In each case, the canine tooth (c.) and the first molar tooth (m.1.) are indicated. Half natural size.

appears to have had its roots in the Aurignacian. The practice of cave art culminated during Magdalenian times in the production of vivid polychrome paintings of animals.

With this very brief summary of the cultural background of human evolution during the Pleistocene Age, let us turn our attention to the fossil evidence of the types of humanity which were responsible for developing the palaeolithic industries. We have seen that some of the early representatives of Man lived in the Far East, where their bony remains have been found in Java and China, and that these ancient precursors of *Homo sapiens* still retained many very primitive features in their skulls, teeth and brains. In Europe, remains of early Man of an approximately equivalent antiquity are represented by the Heidelberg jaw.

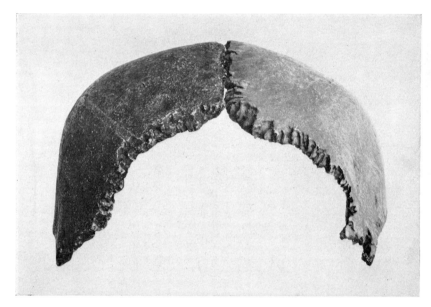

FIG. 34.—Photograph of the left parietal bone of the Swanscombe skull, seen from behind, and placed in apposition to the right parietal bone of a modern European skull. About half natural size. The two bones appear closely similar in size and shape except that the fossil bone is much thicker.

Heidelberg Man (*Homo heidelbergensis*) is known only by a single lower jaw found in 1907 in a sand pit at Mauer, near Heidelberg. It was recovered from a river deposit and was associated with bones and teeth of horse, rhinoceros ("*Rhinoceros*" *etruscus*), *Elephas antiquus*, and other mammals which are characteristic of the early part of the Pleistocene. It probably dates from the commencement of the first interglacial period, which would give it an antiquity of not much less than half a million years. No undoubted stone artifacts were found with the fossil.

The jaw is remarkable for its massive build and for the complete absence of a chin eminence (Fig. 33). This latter

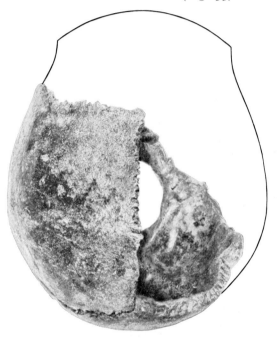

FIG. 35.—The occipital and left parietal bones of the Swanscombe skull, articulated together and seen from above. They have been superimposed on an average contour constructed from the top view of a number of modern human skulls. Note how closely the Swanscombe fossil fits in with the outline of the modern skulls. Half natural size. (Adapted from illustrations in "Report on the Swanscombe Skull," *Journ. Roy. Anthrop. Inst.*, LXVIII, 1938.)

character gives it a somewhat simian appearance. The great width of the hinder ascending part of the jaw (the vertical ramus) and the shallowness of the notch in its upper border are also primitive features, indicating a powerful development of one of the jaw muscles, the masseter muscle. On the other hand, the teeth are fundamentally of the human type. They are large by the average standards

of to-day, but rather small in comparison with the great
size of the jaw itself. The canine teeth are neither unusually
large nor prominent. We know nothing of the rest of the
skull except for so much as can be inferred from the jaw;
for example, the upper jaw and face must have been massively built, the zygomatic arches must have been unusually
stout to provide attachment for the large masseter muscles,
and probably the eyebrow ridges were strongly developed.
It is necessary to wait till more remains of Heidelberg Man
have been discovered before we can amplify the very fragmentary picture we now have of him. Three lower jaws
similar to the Heidelberg jaw, and also showing resemblances to those of *Homo erectus*, have been discovered
at Ternifine in Algeria in association with stone implements of
an early Acheulian industry. A skull cap showing resemblances to *Homo erectus* has also been found recently at Olduvai,
embedded in a Middle Pleistocene stratum some way above the
geological level containing australopithecine remains. It was
associated with palaeolithic implements of the Chellean type

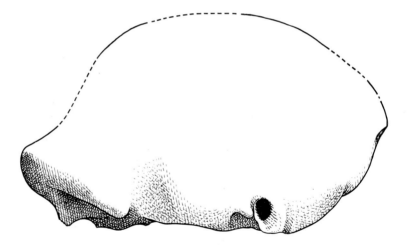

Fig. 36.—Outline of a side view of a Chellean skull, partially reconstructed found at Olduvai in Tanganyika. Approximately
half natural size. Compare this with the outlines of *Homo
erectus* skulls shown in fig. 29. (From a published photograph
by Dr. L. S. B. Leakey.)

and has been dated fairly reliably at about half a million years. In its general appearance it resembles some of the skull caps of *Homo erectus* found in the Far East, though stated to be somewhat larger in its over-all dimensions and, as reconstructed, appears to have a higher forehead (compare Fig. 36 and Fig. 29). The fact that the dating of this Olduvai cranium corresponds closely to that of *Homo erectus* strongly favours the provisional conclusion that it belongs to the same group of early Man. All these fossils suggest that primitive hominids of the *Homo erectus* type may have been widespread over the Old World during the middle part of the Pleistocene. It is particularly interesting to note the remarkable gradational sequence of fossils discovered in East Africa—a temporal as well as a morphological sequence—leading from the generalized ape *Proconsul* in the Miocene, to *Ramapithecus* in the Pliocene, to *Australopithecus* in the Lower Pleistocene, and to men resembling the *Homo erectus* type in the Middle Pleistocene. It may well be, therefore, as Darwin suggested many years ago, that the main line of hominid evolution actually took place on the African continent.

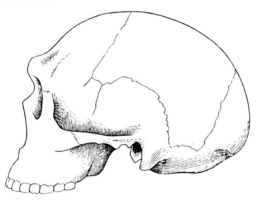

FIG. 37.—The Steinheim skull seen from the side (partly restored). About one-third natural size.

An interesting discovery of early Man was made some years ago in a gravel pit at Swanscombe in Kent. The material comprises three skull bones, the occipital and two parietals, associated with *Elephas antiquus*, *Rhinoceros* and red deer. With them were also found flint implements of such characteristic form that they can be assigned to the middle part of the Acheulian phase of palaeolithic culture. On the geological evidence, the evidence of the flint implements, and the evidence of the associated mammalian remains, it can be stated with a high degree of assurance that the human skull bones date from an interglacial period (probably the terminal part of the second interglacial), which gives it a very considerable antiquity.

While the evidence for its antiquity appears to be reasonably complete, the Swanscombe skull itself is unfortunately very incomplete, but the three bones which have been found are in an exceptionally good state of preservation. Since the sutures (the irregular junctional lines by which one skull bone articulates with the other) are still unobliterated, the skull is evidently that of a young individual of twenty to twenty-five years. Except for their unusual thickness, in which character they are very similar to some other ancient skulls, the bones are quite closely comparable with those of a modern human skull (Figs. 34 and 35). The total volume of the brain—as inferred by comparative studies of modern human skulls whose parietal and occipital bones show similar dimensions and curvatures—is estimated to have been rather more than 1300 c.c., i.e. close to the average size of the human brain to-day. Moreover, an endocranial cast shows that the convolutional pattern made by the foldings of the grey matter on the surface of the brain was just as complicated. The occipital bone is rather unusually broad, but like the other dimensions of the back part of the skull, it falls within the extreme range of variation of modern human skulls.

We have no sure evidence regarding the construction of the front part of the Swanscombe skull. There is some reason to suppose that the face and jaws may have been rather heavily built, for at the front end of the basal portion of the occipital bone is the impression of one of the air sinuses of the nose, indicating that the air sinus system must have been extensively developed. For the same reason it seems probable that the brow ridges may have been strongly built. On the other hand, if any of the features of the face and frontal region had been of an extreme type, they would certainly be reflected in the anatomy of the occipital and parietal bones.

In summary, it may be stated that, *on the evidence of the three bones available*, the remains of the Swanscombe skull suggest that there was a type of Acheulian (or Pre-Mousterian) Man in Europe not markedly different in anatomical features from *Homo sapiens*. If this conclusion is correct, *Homo sapiens* as a species must be considerably more ancient than was at one time supposed.

Another fossil skull which may be as ancient as the Swanscombe skull, and which resembles the latter in certain metrical features, was found at Steinheim in Germany in 1933. However, there is some uncertainty about the antiquity of this fossil; it probably dates either from the second or the third interglacial period. Even if the latter date should eventually prove to be correct, the antiquity of the skull must be very great. The front part of the skull presents a number of primitive features, notably the powerfully developed and prominent brow ridges and the strongly built upper jaw (Fig. 37). By contrast the back part of the skull is rounded and well filled out, as in modern human skulls, and the muscular ridges on the occipital bone do not show the exaggerated development which is such a conspicuous feature of the primitive *Homo erectus* skull. In general, however, the Steinheim skull does suggest an anatomical link between *Homo erectus* and *Homo sapiens*, though approximating much more closely to the latter. The brain capacity is estimated to have been not much more than 1000 c.c., the prominent eyebrow ridges are reminiscent, in a much less pronounced form, of the great supra-orbital excrescence of *Homo erectus*, the forehead region gives the appearance of beginning to fill out while still poorly developed by modern standards, the build of the upper jaw seems to represent a stage of transition from the massive *Homo erectus* jaw to the more refined dimensions characteristic of *Homo sapiens*, while the pointed and angular contour of the occipital region in the *Homo erectus* skull has now been replaced by the rounded contour of modern human skulls.

Somewhat similar to the Steinheim skull, but showing a still closer resemblance to the modern human skull, is a cranium found at Ehringsdorf, near Weimar, in Germany, in 1928. This skull was found associated with early Mousterian implements and with remains of a fauna and flora of warm climate type. Its chronological level can be fairly definitely assigned to the second half of the last interglacial period. The skull has a high vault, a well-developed forehead, a prominent rounded occipital region, and a brain capacity of about 1450 c.c. (Fig. 38). On the other hand, the eyebrow ridges are strongly built and the lower jaw preserves some primitive features, such as the retreating character of the chin.

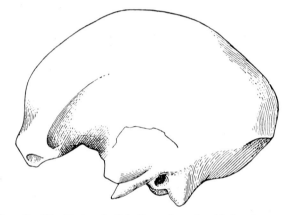

Fig. 38.—The Ehringsdorf skull seen from the side (partly restored) About one-third natural size.

Other fossil skulls which probably date from the latter part of the last interglacial period have been found at Fonté-chevade (in France), Krapina (in Croatia) and at Mount Carmel (in Palestine). In South Africa, also, a human skull was found in 1932 in a peaty, spring deposit at Florisbad, not far from Bloemfontein, which may have been contemporaneous with some of the fossil European skulls just mentioned.

There is a common tendency to assign fossil skulls of great antiquity to distinct species of *Homo*, even though the anatomical basis for such a distinction is not always very convincing. The Steinheim skull, for example, has been the occasion for creating a new species, *Homo steinheimensis*. It is very doubtful, however, whether this skull, or the Swanscombe and Ehringsdorf skulls, can be legitimately distinguished from *Homo sapiens*, particularly if account is taken of the more primitive races of mankind which exist to-day. Similarly, the Fontéchevade and Florisbad skulls appear to be closely similar to modern human skulls. On the other hand, those found at Krapina and Mount Carmel show a considerable variability, particularly in the degree of development of the forehead region and the eyebrow-ridges, but, even so, it does not seem possible on these characters alone to separate them from *Homo sapiens*. Thus it now seems probable that *Homo sapiens*, or at least a type of Man not markedly different from *Homo sapiens*, had already appeared during the second or third interglacial period, contemporaneously with the development of a palaeolithic industry of the Acheulian type, that is to say, in Pre-Mousterian times. Moreover, at least one of these skulls, the Steinheim skull, shows in the forehead region definite traces of an ancestry of the *Homo erectus* type.

There are other fossil human skulls which have sometimes been claimed as evidence of the great antiquity of *Homo sapiens*, such as the Galley Hill skull discovered in 1888 in gravels of the 100-foot terrace of the Thames, and a skull discovered at Bury St. Edmunds apparently in association with Acheulian implements. But the geological evidence for the antiquity of the latter is now discredited and the former is regarded as a later burial.

As a matter of considerable interest, reference may be made to the famous "Piltdown skull" which was recently exposed as a most skilful forgery. The remains, which were reported to have been found in a gravel deposit at Piltdown in Sussex between 1908 and 1915, consisted mainly of pieces of a brain-case very similar to that of modern Man (but remarkable for their thickness), and part of a lower jaw which in its general characters appeared to be indistinguishable from that of a large ape. Some anatomists who were convinced that the skull bones and jaw belonged to the same individual regarded them as the remains of an extremely primitive type of hominid—a sort of "missing link". But others refused to accept this conclusion, and in recent years (particularly since it has been demonstrated that the Piltdown deposits are by no means as ancient as had first been supposed) anthropologists had become increasingly sceptical in their attitude towards "Piltdown Man". Finally, as the result of a most searching examination, it was shown that, while the skull bones may possibly be those of a prehistoric representative of *Homo sapiens*, the jaw bone fragment actually belongs to a modern ape (almost certainly an orang-utan) which had been deliberately faked to give it a fossilized appearance. For students of fossil Man, this investigation of the Piltdown remains was of particular importance because it emphasized the need for the greatest care in the study of fossils alleged to be of great antiquity. But it was even more important because, by demonstrating the application of modern techniques (such as microchemical tests, X-ray spectrography, and crystallographic analysis) in the study of fossil bones, it has now made it virtually impossible for anyone to perpetrate a similar hoax in the future. The details of the methods used in the detection of the Piltdown forgery will be found in the Bulletin of the British Museum (Natural History), Geology, vol. 2, no. 3 (1953) and no. 6 (1955).

An important discovery was made in 1942 at Olorgesailie in the Great Rift Valley of East Africa of quantities of Acheulian hand-axes. No human skeletal remains have as yet been found there, so that it is not known whether the makers of these implements were similar to the types of palaeolithic Man which existed in Europe in Acheulian times. The sites of this discovery, which were evidently camping sites, consist of sedimentary formations deposited on the shores of a lake which existed in the Middle Pleistocene period. Associated with these stone implements have been found the remains of a very interesting assortment of extinct mammals—*Elephas antiquus*, *Hippopotamus gorgops* (a hippopotamus with curious periscopic eyes), *Notochoerus* (a gigantic pig, some species of which were as large as a present-day rhinoceros), *Sivatherium* (a member of the giraffe family with large palmate antlers), and *Simopithecus* (a genus of giant baboons). Acheulian Man in East Africa evidently hunted these animals and used them for food, for the limb bones had clearly been split open to extract the marrow. No burnt bones or traces of hearths have been found at Olorgesailie, and it appears probable, therefore, that the people occupying the camp sites were not acquainted with the use of fire for domestic purposes.

If the Acheulian phase of palaeolithic industry in East Africa was contemporaneous with that in Europe, this sort of evidence seems to indicate than many thousands of years ago large and well organized communities of Man were already living in this region. The possibility also arises that Acheulian Man developed his characteristic culture here and later spread to other parts of the world. Archaeologists, therefore, look forward with eager anticipation to the results of further explorations of Acheulian sites in East Africa.

NEANDERTHAL MAN

The Mousterian phase of palaeolithic culture, which followed the Acheulian and lasted in Europe during the advance of the last glacial period to its climax, was marked by the appearance of a very distinctive type of Man. This type is commonly called Neanderthal Man (or *Homo neanderthalensis*) for the reason that the first described example consisted of skeletal remains which were found in a cave in a valley

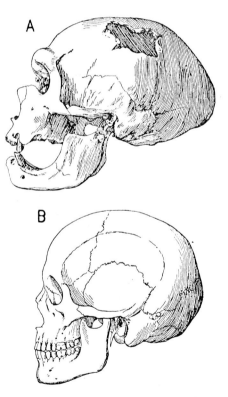

FIG. 39.—The Neanderthal skull of La Chapelle-aux-Saints (A) compared with a modern human skull (B). One-quarter natural size.

of that name, near Düsseldorf in Germany. The type has also been called *Homo mousteriensis*, because of the common association of his skeletal remains with stone implements of the Mousterian industry.

Of the skeleton in the Neanderthal cave, only the top of the skull and a few ribs and limb bones have been preserved. The skull differs from modern human skulls in the enormous development of the brow ridges, the receding forehead, and the flatness of the skull roof. In all these characters it has

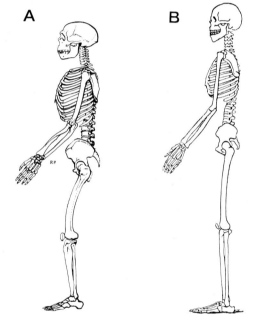

A   **B**

Fig. 40.—Diagrammatic reconstruction of (A) the skeleton of Neanderthal Man, based mainly on that found at La Chapelle-aux-Saints, compared with (B) a modern human skeleton.

a distinctly simian appearance. Part of a smaller skull of the same type had been found as early as 1848 in a cave at Gibraltar, though its significance was only fully realized later. In this skull, also, the huge brow ridges immediately attract attention, and the preservation of the facial region shows that the jaws were massive, the nose unusually broad, and the orbits very large.

Until 1886 the geological age of the Gibraltar and the original Neanderthal remains was uncertain, but in that year two more skeletons of the Neanderthal type were found at Spy, near Namur in Belgium, and in this case they were directly associated with typical Mousterian implements and the bones of mammals (including the mammoth and woolly rhinoceros) characteristic of the last glacial period. The two skulls are more complete than the original Neanderthal fragment, and they show the same characteristic brow ridges and retreating forehead. The lower jaw is remarkable for the absence of a chin eminence and for its massive build. It is reminiscent of the Heidelberg jaw, but the distinctive features of the latter are not developed to such an exaggerated degree.

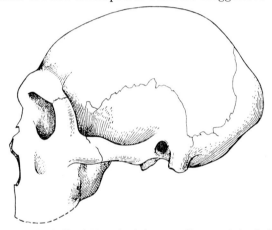

FIG. 41.—A skull of Neanderthal type, discovered in Italy at Monte Circeo (after A. C. Blanc), side view. About one-third natural size.

In 1908 another skeleton was found at La Chapelle-aux-Saints in the south-west of France (Figs. 39 and 40). It was excellently preserved, and sufficiently complete to provide detailed information on the structure of the skull and almost the entire skeleton. The body had been buried in a contracted position in a hollow in the cave floor, and the overlying earth contained numerous broken bones of the woolly rhinoceros, bison, reindeer and other mammals, besides flint implements of characteristic Mousterian shape. There is evidence that the leg of a bison found close to the human skeleton must have been buried while the flesh was still on it, and it is suggested, therefore, that it may have been intended as food for the departed spirit.

Besides the specimens mentioned above, remains which have been ascribed to Neanderthal Man have been found at numerous other sites in Europe and adjacent regions, including the Channel Islands (St. Brelade's Bay, Jersey), Italy (Monte Circeo and Saccopastore), Palestine, South Russia, Siberia, and North Africa. All this accumulation of fossil material has served to emphasize the relative homogeneity of the Neanderthal group, to demonstrate its distinction from modern representatives of *Homo sapiens*, and to show its wide geographical range.

The main anatomical features of typical skulls of Neanderthal Man are as follows (Figs. 39, 40 and 41). The skull as a whole is of large size, with thick cranial walls. The brow ridges are relatively huge, forming a massive shelf of bone overhanging the orbits; the forehead is markedly retreating; the brain-case is flattened in a characteristic fashion; the bony ridges on the occipital bone are powerfully developed for the attachment of exceptionally strong neck muscles; the occipital region of the skull projects backwards in an angular contour; the orbits and nasal aperture are large; the upper jaw is prominent and massively built, and has an inflated appearance related to the large size of the air sinuses which it contains; the palate is broad and capacious; the axis of the foramen magnum on the base of the skull is more deflected from the vertical than in *Homo sapiens*, suggesting a forward tilt of the head on the top of the spine; the lower jaw has a receding chin, and a broad ascending ramus for the attachment of a strong masseter muscle; the teeth are relatively large, and the molars tend in some cases to have unusually large pulp cavities combined with fusion of the roots (a condition called "taurodontism").

The anatomy of the rest of the skeleton also shows many interesting features. For example, the spinous processes of the neck vertebrae are unusually long for the attachment of the powerful neck muscles, and the limb bones have a clumsy appearance with thick curved shafts and disproportionately large extremities. Although the stature of Neanderthal Man hardly exceeded five feet, he was undoubtedly powerful and muscular.

If we now consider Neanderthal Man simply from the

anatomical point of view, it seems obvious that in many of his distinctive features (such as the heavy brow-ridges, the retreating forehead, the large jaws and the shape of some of the limb bones) he appears at first sight to be more ape-like than *Homo sapiens*. Indeed, by some authorities he was at one time taken to represent a stage in the evolution of *Homo sapiens* from ape-like ancestors, and was therefore commonly referred to as *Homo primigenius* (or primaeval Man). The discovery of human remains of pre-Mousterian date, however, has thrown serious doubt on this conception. As we have seen, the fossil evidence now available shows that in pre-Mousterian times there were already in existence human beings of the *Homo sapiens* type, or at least much more closely akin to *Homo sapiens* than Neanderthal Man. In contrast with the coarse construction of some of the Neanderthal limb bones, we know that limb bones of modern human type, without these unusual features, had already been acquired by the primitive *Homo erectus* at a much earlier phase of the Pleistocene period. These facts lead to the inference that, after all, Neanderthal Man does not represent an intermediate stage in the evolution of *Homo sapiens*; rather, he was an aberrant side-line of evolution, the result of a sort of evolutionary retrogression, which manifested itself in an exaggerated development of certain features having only a secondary resemblance to similar features in the anthropoid apes.

There are other facts which lend support to this conclusion. For example, some of the distinctive features of Neanderthal Man, such as the tendency towards a taurodontism of the molar teeth and the over-development of the brow ridges, appear to be somewhat specialized characters peculiar to this group. Again, if the various remains of Neanderthal Man are placed in their chronological sequence, it appears that some of the earlier fossils, dating from the earlier part of the Mousterian period, are less "Neanderthaloid" in their skeletal characters (and thus approximate more closely to *Homo sapiens*) than the extreme Neanderthal type of later date. The fact, also that no fossil remains of a date *later* than the Mousterian have been found which mark a transition to *Homo sapiens* suggests very strongly that at the end of the Mousterian period (i.e. before the latter part of the last glaciation of the Ice Age) the extreme type of Neanderthal Man became extinct.

Whether the extreme type of Neanderthal Man is properly to be regarded as a species distinct from *Homo sapiens* has been a matter of dispute. We take the view here that a specific distinction, under the designation of *Homo neanderthalensis*, is warranted partly because the contrast it shows in anatomical structure with *Homo sapiens* appears to equate well with the degree of contrast between different species of other higher Primates, and largely on the grounds of the statistical studies of G. M. Morant which led him to the conclusion that the available measurements of the skulls of Neanderthal Man not only show that the type was remarkably homogeneous, but that "between it and all modern types there is a distinct hiatus, which may be taken to indicate a specific difference".

We have mentioned (p. 102) the variability of the skulls found at Mount Carmel and Krapina, some approximating to the typical Neanderthal type and others approximating more closely to modern *Homo sapiens*. It has even been suggested that the Mount Carmel population was the result of inter-breeding between Neanderthal Man and *Homo sapiens*. If this were the case, it would be a strong argument against accepting a specific distinction for Neanderthal Man. But this hypo-thesis of interbreeding seems to have been based on the assumption that the individuals whose remains have been found at each of these localities lived contemporaneously. In the case of the Mount Carmel site, however, there is evidence that this was occupied over a prolonged period of time, perhaps as much as ten thousand years. It may reasonably be sug-gested, therefore, that the Mount Carmel caves were successively occupied by shifting populations at a time when pre-Mousterian types closely akin in anatomical characters to modern Man were undergoing an evolutionary differentiation into the definitive species *Homo sapiens* on the one hand, and on the other, into the extreme Neanderthal type, *Homo neander-thalensis*.

Reference should be made to the brain of Neanderthal Man, so far as its shape and size can be studied from endocranial casts of the fossil skulls. Although in its general shape it shows certain features of primitive appearance, in size it was large. Indeed, the average size of the brain (about 1450 c.c.) was rather larger than the average size of the modern human brain (1350 c.c.) though there is a considerable overlap in the range of variation between the two types. We know nothing of the quality of the Neanderthal brain, apart from what may be inferred indirectly from a study of the Mousterian culture; but the fact that it attained such a large average size makes it less easy to fit in to a scheme of the evolution of the brain of *Homo sapiens*, and thus provides additional evidence that Neanderthal Man was not on the direct line of evolution of modern Man.

There is no doubt that discussions in the past on the evolutionary significance of Neanderthal Man have to some extent been confused by a lack of precise definition of the term "Neanderthal". Some authorities, for example, would regard the Steinheim and Ehringsdorf fossils as early representatives of "Neanderthal Man" because of the strong brow ridges, even though the latter do not reach the great development of typical Mousterian Man of later date, and though other features, such as those of the forehead and occipital regions, do not show the typical Neanderthal characters (and thus are more comparable with *Homo sapiens*). Now, we have seen that early Mousterian Man was in some cases less "Neanderthaloid" than later Mousterian Man. It is thus convenient to refer to the latter as the *extreme Neanderthal type*, showing a gross exaggeration of the brow ridges, a large brain, and the development of specializations such as taurodontism. The earlier type, in which the brow ridges, though strongly developed, did not reach such extreme proportions, while the skull as a whole showed more of the refinements of *Homo sapiens* and the brain was of smaller size, may then be called the *generalized Neanderthal type*. The Steinheim and Ehringsdorf skulls approximate to the latter type, and may perhaps, therefore, be legitimately included in this category.

Using this terminology, we can now make the following provisional statement on the evolution of *Homo sapiens*. It has already been noted that the brain size of *Homo erectus* showed a considerable variability, in some cases reaching well within the range of variation in modern Man. It may be inferred that a progressive development of the brain in the *Homo erectus* type of early Man would have led eventually to the appearance of a generalized Neanderthal type of Man. At this point in the evolutionary history of the *Hominidae*, presumably in Acheulian and Early Mousterian times, two separate lines of development evidently made their appearance. In one of these the continued expansion of the brain was associated with an exaggerated development of the brow ridges, the jaws and palate, certain specializations of the skull and teeth, and retrogressive changes in the limb skeleton, leading eventually to the extreme Neanderthal type associated with the later Mousterian industry. In the other line a progressive enlargement of the brain was associated with a recession of the brow ridges and the jaws, a diminution in the size of the teeth, the construction of a more evenly rounded cranium with a vertical forehead, and the retention of the limb characters already developed much earlier in the *Homo erectus* group. This second line evidently led through Acheulian Man to *Homo sapiens*.

Neanderthaloid Man in Africa and Asia

Men of Neanderthaloid appearance were by no means confined to Europe and adjacent regions in palaeolithic times. They spread to distant parts of the world, where in some cases they probably persisted to a much later period than they did in Europe.

In 1921, in a cave at Broken Hill in N. Rhodesia (Zambia), human remains were found in association with primitive kinds of stone and bone implements, and with the broken bones of animals which had evidently been used for food. The bones belong to types of animal still living in Rhodesia, or to scarcely distinguishable species. Moreover, they appear to be in a remarkably fresh state of preservation, only encrusted with a thin covering of lead and zinc ores. The human remains comprise a nearly complete skull and part of the upper jaw of a slightly smaller skull, portions of limb bones, part of a hip bone and a sacrum. The skull is remarkable for the great size of the facial skeleton, and for the huge brow ridges which in their massive build are unsurpassed by any other known human skulls (Fig. 42). Resemblances are shown to Neanderthal Man in the voluminous appearance of the upper jaw, the wide palate, and the contour of the brain-case as seen from the side. On the other hand, there are certain differences in the construction of the nose and ear parts of the skull, and the foramen magnum shows no backward deflection such as is the case in some of the typical

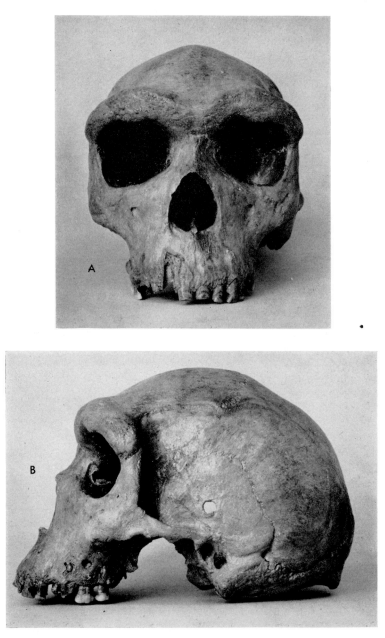

FIG. 42.—The Rhodesian skull, face view (A) and side view (B).
Less than one-half natural size.

Mousterian skulls. The volume of the brain is estimated to have been somewhat less than 1300 c.c.

In contrast with the unusual appearance of the Rhodesian skull, the associated limb bone fragments are not distinguishable from those of *Homo sapiens*. Indeed, the question has arisen whether the limb bones and the skull belong to the same individual. This sort of question is not uncommon in the study of human fossils, where unexpected combinations of anatomical characters are found to occur, but in the present instance there appears to be no sound anatomical reason which forbids the inference that the skull and limb bones form a natural association. It is interesting to record that a spectrographic analysis of small fragments of bone removed from the fossils has been undertaken. It showed that the proportions of minerals with which the bony material has in the course of time become impregnated are consistent with the view that the skull and limb bones came from the same level in the cave deposits; in other words, it gives some support to the conclusion that they are parts of the same or related individuals.

In summary, it is clear that the fossil Man of Rhodesia shows many similarities to Neanderthal Man of Europe, but there are also obvious differences. Because of the latter, some anatomists assign him to a separate species *Homo rhodesiensis.*

The antiquity of Rhodesian Man is not certainly known, for the geological evidence is inconclusive. The associated implements are of later Levalloisian type, but the animal bones found in the cave and the fresh appearance of the skull suggests that the antiquity may not be very great. In this connection, mention may be made of the curious fact that many of the teeth show an advanced degree of dental decay, for such a pathological condition is commonly regarded as a feature of relatively modern times, and is but rarely seen in very ancient skulls.

In 1953, during investigations which were being made by a group of scientists from the University of Cape Town, a skull cap which is almost a replica of that of Rhodesian Man was found at Hopefield near Saldanha Bay, 80 miles north of Cape Town. The cranial capacity of this specimen has been estimated at about 1250 c.c., and the eyebrow ridges are relatively enormous. From the associated stone implements of late Acheulian type and the associated fauna, as well as geological considerations, it has been inferred that the skull probably antedates the last glacial period in Europe. The discovery of "Saldanha Man" is important because it confirms the evidence of Rhodesian Man that there was a

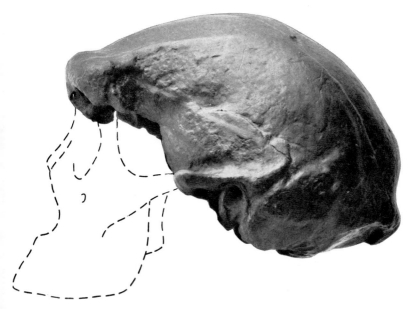

FIG. 43.—One of the crania found at Ngandong in Java (*Homo soloensis*), with a tentative reconstruction of the outline of the face. Approximately half natural size.

rather aberrant type of *Homo* in Africa at the end of the Pleistocene, and because it suggests that this type may have been in existence there over a considerable period of time.

In 1931 and 1932 a series of eleven skulls were found in late Pleistocene deposits in Java, which show some resemblance to the Rhodesian skull. Unfortunately, all these skulls lack the facial skeleton. The brow ridges are thick and strong, and the muscular crests on the occipital bone are particularly well developed (Fig. 43). The foramen magnum occupies a position corresponding to that of *Homo sapiens*. The brain volume appears to have been relatively low, ranging from about 1150 to 1300 c.c. Only one limb bone was found with the skulls, a shin bone (tibia), and this is in all respects comparable to that of modern Man, showing none of the typical Neanderthal characters. These Javanese remains were found at a place called Ngandong on the River Solo, and for this reason the type of early Man which they

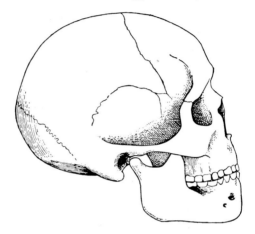

Fig. 44.—A skull of Cro-Magnon type found at Combe-Capelle and dating from Aurignacian times. Approximately one-quarter natural size.

represent has been called *Homo soloensis*. When more complete fossil remains come to light it may be found that the anatomical features of the type are sufficiently distinctive to warrant the creation of a separate species. With the information at present available, however, it appears that, like Rhodesian Man, Solo Man was probably one of the variants of the Neanderthal stock.

Like the extreme Neanderthal type in Europe, there is no doubt that the Rhodesian and Solo types became extinct. They were probably too highly specialized in structure and too late in time to have formed the precursors of any of the modern races of mankind.

HOMO SAPIENS IN LATE PALAEOLITHIC TIMES

At the end of the Mousterian phase of palaeolithic culture, the Neanderthal inhabitants of Europe were abruptly replaced by people of completely modern European type.

There is reason to suppose that this new population, the Aurignacians, having developed their distinctive culture elsewhere, probably in Asia, migrated into Europe and, with their superior social organization, quickly displaced Mousterian Man and occupied his territory.

The remains of some of the Aurignacian people have been found at Cro-Magnon in Southern France. They were a finely built race, tall and muscular, with a high cranial capacity and refined facial features. It would probably have been impossible to distinguish them in life from some of the groups of people which inhabit Europe to-day. In some instances, as, for example, in the Aurignacian skull found at Combe-Capelle in France, the brow ridges were moderately well developed (Fig. 44), but not more so than in many modern skulls.

In a cave at Grimaldi, on the Riviera, two skeletons of Aurignacian age have been found which have a somewhat negroid appearance, particularly in the projecting character of the jaws. It has been argued, indeed, that they represent an incursion into Southern Europe of a negroid race from Africa, and interesting parallels have been drawn between the details of Aurignacian cave paintings and the cave art of the modern Bushman to-day. However, the alleged negroid features of the Grimaldi skeletons have been questioned by some anatomists, and it remains doubtful whether they are sufficiently distinctive to warrant any definite conclusions regarding their racial character.

The period of the Aurignacian culture was followed in some parts of Europe by the Solutrean industry, which was of quite short duration. Then came the Magdalenian period, which lasted for a considerable time and terminated about 10,000 years ago. The period of the Magdalenian culture in Europe was marked by a climate of almost arctic severity, and it is sometimes referred to as the Reindeer Age because of the prevalence of these animals during the period. The interesting feature of the few human remains which have so far been recovered from Magdalenian deposits is that some of them show anatomical characters in which they quite closely resemble the modern Eskimo. This is particularly the case with a skull found at Chancelade, in the Dordogne region of France, which displays Eskimoid features in the shape of the brain-case (with its vertical sides and its "keeled" roof), in the narrowness of the nasal aperture, in the breadth of the cheek region of the face, and in the shape of the lower jaw. It has been argued on the basis of this sort of evidence, as well as on the curious similarities which exist between some elements of the Magdalenian culture and those of the modern Eskimo, that western Europe during Magdalenian times was actually populated by Eskimos. It has further been suggested that, with the retreat of the ice during the terminal phases of the last glaciation, the reindeer migrated northwards and were followed by the Eskimos, who thus found themselves eventually in their present habitat in the arctic regions. However, in certain characters the Chancelade skull shows what appear to be significant differences from the Eskimo, and it may well be nothing more than a variant of the Cro-Magnon type, which is known, from other fossil evidence, to have persisted into the Magdalenian period.

Apart from problems related to the actual racial characters of the population which inhabited Europe during the final phases of the Pleistocene period, there remains no doubt that it was composed of people of completely modern type. *Homo sapiens*, with a highly developed culture, flourished in Europe at least as far back as the beginning of the Aurignacian period, that is, about 35,000 years ago, and well before the termination of the last glaciation of the Ice Age.

GENERAL SUMMARY

We have followed the stages in the progressive evolution of the Primates which culminated in the appearance of human beings. We have seen that it is possible to illustrate, by reference to comparative anatomical and fossil evidence, the gradual transformation of small generalized mammals similar to tree-shrews into the higher Primates, and even into Man himself. Although the fossil record is still far from complete, it is yet sufficient to allow us to link up one evolutionary stage with another in a natural sequence. The gaps which remain in this sequence are no longer of such an order as to demand any great effort of scientific imagination to fill them with hypothetical "missing links." We can readily conceive the transition from a tree-shrew type of ancestor to the primitive lemuroids and tarsioids of Eocene times, from these small Primates to progressive tarsioids with many simian features, from these again to the small gibbon-like animals of the Oligocene, to the larger generalized apes of the Miocene, to the remarkable *Australopithecinae* of South Africa, and to primitive men of the *Homo erectus* group. In later Pleistocene times the transition from these primitive types of Man to Pre-Mousterian Man and Early Mousterian Man is equally easy to follow. Lastly, the evolutionary development from Early Mousterian Man, in one direction to the extreme Neanderthal type that became extinct, and in the other direction to modern *Homo sapiens*, is now well documented in the fossil record (Fig. 45).

No doubt the most conspicuous hiatus in this series lies between the Miocene and Pliocene apes and the *Australopithecinae*. For while we now have numerous fossil remains of the former, they are not yet sufficiently complete to ascertain just how or when a transition from one to the other occurred. At the beginning of Miocene times the early anthropoid apes were splitting up into divergent radiations, some of which evidently gave rise to the ancestors of the existing genera of anthropoid apes. Others, however, by avoiding the peculiar specializations of the modern apes and by the perfection of their limbs for terrestrial progression, may have gradually assumed an upright posture and provided the starting-point for the evolutionary development of the early *Hominidae*. When the skulls and limbs of these particular forms are known in detail, they will furnish evidence of the highest importance for elucidating the evolutionary changes which first led to the appearance of the *Hominidae* as a separate and independent branch of the Hominoidea.

The whole evolutionary history of the Primates has been marked by one special feature which obtrudes itself very forcibly on the attention, and that is the progressive expansion and elaboration of the brain. A gradual increase in the size of the brain since Eocene times also occurred in other groups of mammals, but in the Primates the expansion began earlier, occurred more rapidly, and proceeded further, than in any other mammalian Order. In spite of much speculation, nothing certainly is known of the fundamental cause of this expansion, though there are many reasons for thinking that it was at first favoured and perhaps accelerated by the conditions of existence associated with an arboreal

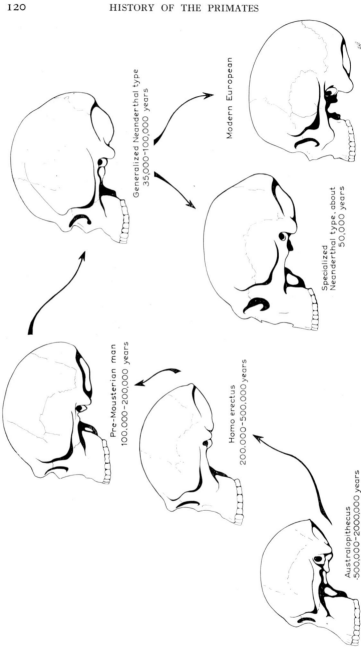

FIG. 45.—Diagram illustrating the appearance of the skull in a
series of fossil hominid types arranged in their temporal sequence.

mode of life. The growth of the brain had an important influence on many other parts of the body, because it permitted the retention of primitive and generalized characters which in many other mammalian groups were lost by structural specialization. This is simply the result of the fact that Primates were able to maintain themselves in the struggle for existence by the exercise of wile and cunning in situations where lowlier and less progressive types of animal were compelled to develop specialized weapons of defence and offence in order to ensure the preservation of their species. The retention by the Primates of primitive anatomical characters in many parts of their body has provided them with a structural plasticity which has been of the utmost importance to them in their evolutionary potentialities. The wile and cunning of the earlier Primates have become the intelligence of the higher Primates, and Man himself has surpassed all other members of the animal kingdom in his capacity for mental activities of the most elaborate kind.

If Man has gained his intellectual dominance over his fellow creatures by concentrating his evolutionary energies on the development of his brain, it remains to be seen whether he can now maintain his position by contriving a method of living in orderly relations with members of his own species. If he fails to do so, he may yet follow the example of many other groups of animals which have achieved a temporary ascendancy by an exaggerated development of some particular structural mechanism. He may become extinct.

LITERATURE

Further details of the subjects discussed in this guide will be found in the following books and papers:

BARNETT, A. 1957. *The Human Species.* 351 pp. London (Pelican).

BOULE, M. & H. V. Vallois. 1957. *Fossil Men.* xxv + 535 pp., 298 text-figs. London.

BOULENGER, E. G. 1936. *Apes and Monkeys.* 236 pp., 30 pls. London.

BRODRICK, A. H. 1948. *Early Man.* 288 pp., 21 pls. London.

BROOM, R., & ROBINSON, J. T. 1952. Swartkrans Ape-Man, *Paranthropus crassidens. Transvaal Mus. Mem.*, **6**: 123 pp., 8 pls.

COLBERT, E. H. 1955. *Evolution of the Vertebrates.* 479 pp., 122 text-figs. New York & London.

Cold Spring Harbor Symposia on Quantitative Biology, **15.** Origin and Evolution of Man. 425 pp. New York, 1950.

COLE, S. 1964. *The Prehistory of East Africa.* 382 pp., 22 pls., 60 text-figs. London.

DOBZHANSKY, T. 1962. *Mankind Evolving.* xiii + 381 pp., 10 text-figs. London.

DARWIN, C. R. 1930. *The Descent of Man.* 10th ed. 244 pp. London.

HARRISON, G. A., WEINER, J. S., TANNER, J. M. & BARNICOT, N. A. 1964. *Human Biology.* vii + 536 pp., 81 text-figs., 2 pls. Oxford.

HOWELL, J. C. 1951. *The Place of Neanderthal Man in Human Evolution,* Amer. Journ. Phys. Anthropol., **9**, 379.

HOWELLS, W. 1959. *Mankind in the Making.* 382 pp. New York.

HOWELLS, W. (Ed.). 1962. *Ideas on Human Evolution,* Selected Essays. 555 pp. Harvard.

HRDLICKA, A. 1930. The Skeletal Remains of Early Man. *Smithson. Misc. Coll.*, Washington, **83**: x + 379 pp., 93 pls.

LEAKEY, L. S. B. 1936. *The Stone Age of Africa.* 218 pp., 13 pls. Oxford.

LE GROS CLARK, W. E. 1964. *The Fossil Evidence of Human Evolution: An Introduction to the Study of Paleo-anthropology.* 2nd ed. xii + 201 pp., 26 text-figs. Chicago.

LE GROS CLARK, W. E. 1962. *The Antecedents of Man.* 2nd ed. vii + 388 pp., 156 text-figs. Edinburgh.

LE GROS CLARK, W. E. & LEAKEY, L. S. B. 1951. The Miocene Hominoidea of East Africa. *Fossil Mammals of Africa.* No. 1. 117 pp., 28 text-figs., 9 pls. British Museum (Nat. Hist.), London.

LE GROS CLARK, W. E., MORANT, G. M., and others. 1938. Report on the Swanscombe Skull. *J. Roy. Anthrop. Inst.*, London, **68**: 17-98, pls. 1-6.

McCOWN, T. D., & KEITH, A. 1939. *The Stone Age of Mount Carmel*, **2.** 390 pp., 28 pls. Oxford.

MONTAGU, M. F. ASHLEY. 1951. *An Introduction to Physical Anthropology.* 555 pp., 160 text-figs. Springfield, U.S.

MOORE, R. 1962. *Man, Time and Fossils.* 2nd ed. 400 pp., 24 pls. London.

MORANT, G. M. 1927. *Studies of Palaeolithic Man. II. A biometric study of Neanderthaloid skulls and their relationships to modern racial types.* Ann. Eugenics, **2**, 318.

NAPIER, J. R. 1959. Fossil Metacarpals from Swartkrans. *Fossil Mammals of Africa*, No. 17. 18 pp., 2 text-figs., 2 pls. British Museum (Nat. Hist.), London.

NAPIER, J. R., & DAVIS, P. R. 1959. The Fore-limb Skeleton and Associated Remains of *Proconsul africanus. Fossil Mammals of Africa*, No. 16. 69 pp., 16 text-figs., 10 pls. British Museum (Nat. Hist.), London.

OAKLEY, K. P. 1961. *Man the Tool-Maker.* 5th ed. 98 pp., 2 pls., 41 text-figs. Brit. Mus. (Nat. Hist.), London.

— 1964. *Frameworks for Dating Fossil Man* x + 355 pp., 82 text figs. London.

— 1964. The Problem of Man's Antiquity: An Historical Survey. *Bull. Brit. Mus. (Nat. Hist.) Geol.*, **9**, 5: 83-155, 3 pls.

OAKLEY, K. P., & MONTAGU, M. F. ASHLEY. 1949. A Reconsideration of the Galley Hill Skeleton. *Bull. Brit. Mus. (Nat. Hist.) Geol.*, **1**, 2: 27-46, pl. 4.

ROBINSON, J. T. 1956. *The Dentition of the Australopithecinae. Transvaal Mus. Mem.*, **22**, pp. 179., 50 text-figs.

ROMER, A. S. 1941. *Man and the Vertebrates.* 3rd ed., ix + 405 pp., 106 pls. Chicago.

SIMONS, E. L. 1963. *A Critical Reappraisal of Tertiary Primates*, from *Evolutionary and Genetic Biology of Primates.* 129 pp., 22 text-figs. Acad. Press.

SIMPSON, G. G. 1945. The Principles of Classification and a Classification of Mammals. *Bull. Amer. Mus. Nat. Hist.*, **85**: 350 pp.

— 1950. *The Meaning of Evolution.* 364 pp., 38 text-figs. Oxford.

STIRTON, R. A. 1959. *Time, Life & Man. The Fossil Record.* xi + 558 pp., 291 text-figs. New York.

WASHBURN, S. L. (Ed.) 1964. *Classification and Human Evolution.* 371 pp. (17 Essays). London.

WEIDENREICH, F. 1943. The Skull of *Sinanthropus pekinensis. Palaeont. Sinica,* Peking (n.s., D), **10.** 298 pp., 93 pls.

WEINER, J. S., OAKLEY, K. P. & LE GROS CLARK, W. E. 1953. The Solution of the Piltdown Problem. *Bull. Brit. Mus. (Nat. Hist.) Geol.,* **2**: 3, 139-146, pls. 8, 9.

WEINER, J. S., and others. 1955. Further Contributions to the Solution of the Piltdown Problem. *Bull. Brit. Mus. (Nat. Hist.) Geol.,* **2,** 6: 225-287, pls. 27-31.

ZEUNER, F. E. 1952. *Dating the Past.* 3rd ed. 495 pp., 24 pls. London.

INDEX

An asterisk (*) indicates a figure.